INVE$T
REINVE$T
RE$T

INVESTMENT ADVICE FOR
ALL GENERATIONS

SONJA M. HAGGERT

Haggert Business Solutions, LLC
PO Box 98
West Point, PA 19486
www.sonjahaggert.com

Ordering information:
Quantity sales. Special discounts are available on quantity purchases by corporations, associations, and others. For details, contact the "Special Sales Department" at the address above.

ISBN   978-0-692-16622-2 (paperback)
            978-0-692-17887-4 (ebook)

Library of Congress Cataloging-in-Publication Data:
Haggert, Sonja
        Invest, Reinvest, Rest Investment Advice for all Generations-1st ed. Investments. 2.
        Finance, Personal. 3. Title.

Book design by Darlene Swanson • www.van-garde.com

This book is dedicated to all those folks out there who say to me, "I wish I had known this sooner." You can still do this!

This book is also dedicated to the very special people in my life; my husband, Brian, whose support made this book possible and our nieces, Carolyn and Kristen, who bring a great deal of joy to our lives.

Contents

Is This Book For You?

This book is for you if...

- You aren't making enough money with a CD, savings, or checking account.

- You never had a course about investing in school.

- Financial information makes your eyes glaze over.

- You don't want to read ten books—or even five—about "how to invest."

- You think that you are educated about investing, but the results aren't there.

- You fully trust someone else with your finances but want to be able to carry on an intelligent conversation about your situation.

- YOU ARE A WOMAN

There, now, have I covered most of you?

Do you want to add to the list some concerns about financial institutions, since they are getting some bad press? Well, go right ahead!

You may be wondering if you can find information somewhere out there to guide you that:

1. won't cost a fortune,

2. will make you some real money, and

3. will not require you to become an expert.

Yes, yes, and yes!

This book will show you where to go to get worthwhile and unbiased information that you can use on your own or in conjunction with a financial adviser.

Like you, I too wanted to make money with my stock investments without having to get a separate college degree.

Why should you care about investing?

Because you're a woman and you're worth it!

Ok, whether you like it or not, you will have to manage your finances and perhaps those of family members at some point in your life. If you're doing it now, great! But are you participating or just listening to the man or adviser in your life "who knows better?"

Women live longer than men so whatever assets we have must work harder to last longer.

Women want to be treated equally with men, and receive commensurate pay, but often choose to delegate financial responsibility to someone else.

What do you do when a crisis strikes and you are suddenly in charge of finances?

Did I get your attention?

If you're managing your own investments, how's that going for you? Are you making the average annual return of 7% that you would make with stocks? How do you pick stocks in which to invest? Is it the latest sexy trend or technology? Do you have a plan or just let your adviser make the decisions?

For the men out there who have chosen to read this book, just like women, you should care about investing.

Because it's **your** money and no one will care about it like **you**!

We all need a plan for life's events, not only retirement but a new car, or a bigger house because your family is growing, or a second house in your favorite place. Most important, if you have someone managing your money, you need to know if he or she is doing a good job—not just because he or she says so or tells you in a language you don't understand.

Let's face it—you know how to get the best cell-phone plan, how to get a good deal at the grocery store, and who makes the best pizza in the area. Shouldn't you know if you're making real money or just paying a lot of fees for not so much return?

When my husband and I started to invest on our own without an adviser, I wanted to learn as much as possible, so I started reading the financial pages. I had to anyway because I ran a manufacturing company and was responsible for managing profit and loss. But that didn't help with my investments. If anything, it was a hindrance in that it didn't take into account the nuances that make up the investment world. There are many!

What I learned was, it's not that hard if you follow some very important ground rules. It took me several years to discover and trust them, and I want to share them with you.

This book is about where to find unbiased research to help you make the most informed stock picks. If you think that's the next sexy technology company or your favorite online store, I hope you'll re-think that when you've read this book.

I'm sticking to stocks because they

- are cheap,
- require minimal time,
- can be bought with limited funds,
- achieve excellent results, and
- limit your risk.

This is possible thanks to discount brokers, advice from the right people, and as little as $2000 in starting funds. The two big takeaways are, the importance of compounding and trailing stops.

You'll read about Judy's compounding success that turned $2000 into $7,000,000 in forty-six years.

Here is a great story from the article "Want Your Kids to Be Rich? Do This" in *The Oxford Club Communique* (May 1, 2013). In the section "The Magic of Compounding," Marc Lichtenfeld writes,

"...Let's take a look at a theoretical example...investing $10,000 for my eight-year-old today.

The portfolio [the stocks that Marc has bought for his daughter] has a current yield of 4% (makes 4% a year) and the dividends are raised by an average of 10% per year. [Unlike CD's at the bank that tend to go up only when interest rates go up, companies can increase their dividend (payout to you) when they decide to do so. [Some of the best companies do this on a regular basis].

In 10 years the $10,000 grows into $31,777. Not bad. It'll help pay for a year in college.

But because of her extraordinary intellect (she clearly takes after her dad), [Reminder: this is Marc speaking], she's offered a full scholarship, so no tuition is needed. Instead she doesn't touch the money and continues to let it grow. After 20 years she has $113,019, perhaps enough for a down payment on a house. And she's only 28 years old. A nice little nest egg before she's even hit 30.

But instead of buying a house, she decides to take over the old homestead after my wife and I downsize to a condo. Since she doesn't need the down payment, she lets the money grow for another 10 years.

Now at 38 years old, she's sitting on a nest egg worth $463,089. She's got some kids of her own now (the grandkids are so cute, you should see their pictures!) and she's saving for their college tuitions, so she lets it ride for another 10 years.

Now at age 48, she's got $2,266,598 in her account, spinning off $196,359 in annual income—all from an initial investment of $10,000, and 40 years in time."

Can you picture this for your kids or grandkids?

You don't want to lose what you've earned so you'll get to know trailing stops as a fail-safe way to sell, or limit potential downsides so you don't lose more than you're comfortable with.

You'll have to read on for the details.

This book is short and to the point. There aren't a lot of stories. Stories are for novels. It tells you where to go to get the best information when it comes to investing in stocks.

Lastly, I think investing should have an aspect of fun. When was the last time you traveled to a great place and were able to write it off on your taxes? As an investor you could be relaxing in the sun after a morning seminar and get a tax break.

As I am writing this, it looks like the Tax Cuts and Jobs Act of 2017 will eliminate these deductions dealing a blow to small investors. But tax laws change and taking advantage of learning opportunities is worth it.

I hope you enjoy investing in stocks as much as I do. At a minimum, you'll find your conversations with your investment professional much more stimulating and worthwhile.

## CHAPTER 1

Why Buy Stocks?

"Because stocks are a living, breathing entity that will astonish, irritate and challenge you and always give you something to talk about." —Sonja Haggert

The purpose of this book is to show you how choosing the right financial newsletter can make stock picking easy for any investor, especially the novice.

So why buy stocks?
Because they are cheap, easy, and liquid, and with the right discipline, they can provide excellent results.

What is a stock?
The business dictionary defines it as follows: A share of a company held by an individual or group. Corporations raise capital by issuing stocks and entitle stock owners (shareholders) to partial ownership

of the corporation. Stocks are bought and sold on what is called an exchange. There are several types of stocks and the two most typical forms are preferred stock and common stock.

OK, let's skip the jargon and call it ownership in a company.

> **Stock:** *Owning stock in a company means you have a share in the ownership of that company.*

Stocks are real companies with real people where you and your neighbors and friends work. They add to the economy and can be part of the service or manufacturing industries, for example.

Companies reflect the personalities of their CEOs (good and bad) and the people who work there. Part of their purpose as a public company is to make the shareholders happy by increasing the value of the company's stock and having and/or growing the dividend (a payout some companies make during the year).

Public companies are required to have annual meetings to give an update on how the company is doing. As a shareholder, you will be able to vote on items on the agenda, and you are welcome to attend these meetings.

Just because a company is large doesn't necessarily mean it is a public company, and you can purchase stock. Companies, such as Dell Computer and Albertson's Super Markets, have chosen to remain private and not invite investors into their business.

Wait, I Need an Example of Why Investing In a Stock Is So Great.

Let's compare it to your bank statement.

With a bank account, you get interest once a month. Period—that's it. Not much to capture your attention. No great new discovery, no super-sale event—just a few cents or dollars. Worse yet, if you buy a six-month timed certificate of deposit (CD), you have to wait six months for that measly amount of interest.

> ***Certificate of deposit (CD):*** *According to Google, a CD is issued by a bank to a person depositing money for a specific period of time. A timed CD is one in which the depositor can only make a withdrawal by giving notice.*

With a stock, you have the possibility that a share of stock you bought at $10 will go up to $11. And if that stock has a dividend, you will get additional monies either quarterly or twice a year. You can decide to buy a stock on Monday and sell it on Wednesday (I wouldn't recommend this), and unlike a CD, your money is not locked up.

Let's say you bought one hundred shares of a $10 stock ($1,000), and it went up to $11 (now worth $1,100). If it stays there until you sell it, you made $100.

Now let's say that stock has a quarterly **dividend** of $0.05/share. That means four times a year, you will be paid $5 or an additional $20. And that's a check or a deposit into your account (or better yet, reinvested; we'll talk about that later)—yes, real money.

If you don't sell the stock, that money more than likely will just keep coming.

(Unless there is a problem with the company, most companies do not like to lower or, worse yet, eliminate their dividend.) It's possible that the price of the stock will also go up.

Are you starting to see how good this can get?

> **Dividend:** *A dividend is a payment made by the company to its investors. This is often in cash but can be in shares of stock. It usually comes from the earnings of a company.*

Let's say you left that stock alone, and after a year and a day, you decided to sell it. (I use that time frame to show you what is considered a "long-term gain"—more than one year.) You made $120 on that stock ($100 from the share price and $20 in dividends). That's **12 percent!** I don't know about your bank, but mine isn't paying those types of rates now. Best of all, because this is considered a long-term gain, you probably won't pay the standard income tax rate on the sale but a long-term dividend tax rate of about 15 percent.[1] Talk about a win-win.

Wait, I'm Not Taking a Course On Stock Investing!

So, maybe I've got your interest piqued, and you decide that having stocks would be a good idea. But you don't want to learn all the jargon; you don't want to be tied to your computer, or maybe you don't know where to start. Maybe you'll hire someone to do the work for you. That's fine too. But how do you find someone, and how do you determine if his or her goals are the same as yours?

Well, I think there's a better way, a way you can "have your cake and eat it too." That's what this book is about. Yes, there are people who will be helping you make choices of what to buy and sell. They will even tell you when to buy and sell, and you won't have to learn any of the jargon. Interested?

> **Financial newsletter:** *A publication that provides investment research to enable an investor to make an informed buying or selling decision. Newsletters may be mailed, faxed, or available online. They may arrive monthly, weekly, or at other intervals, depending upon the editor. There are many free ones available that are used to pique interest in subscription, fee-based publications. Those fee-based publications may run from under a hundred to hundreds or thousands of dollars.*

My intent is to help you find the best, most reasonable one, for your purpose.

I want to introduce you to **financial newsletters.** Some of these are written by the smartest guys and gals in the business. It's not just me saying that, either…the *Wall Street Journal* and other reliable sources are saying it too!

These financial newsletters will tell you when to buy and, much more important, *when to sell.* Some newsletters will send an alert to your computer and/or smartphone so that you'll be on top of the information when it hits.

If the information you receive from the financial newsletters isn't enough to satisfy you, Yahoo Finance provides a ton of valuable information to investors (you and me) for *free.* Most public companies also have a website that includes investor information with ways to call, e-mail, or write for more information. Just like with the products they sell, **public companies** want your business as an investor.

> **Public companies**: *Companies that sell stock, allowing you to invest in their business.*

What's This Going to Cost Me?

This is the best part. Buying stocks has never been cheaper. You can do it yourself through a discount broker who charges as little as $9.99. There are specials that may be lower than this, with some brokerages offering trades for free. There is an app, Robinhood, that is always free except for US Securities and Exchange Commission (SEC) fees. However, if you do pay a fee to buy and sell, it may be tax deductible. The same with the cost of the newsletter.

You don't have to buy the most expensive stocks. You can buy quality stocks for $10 to $20. And you can start with as little as $2,000, $5,000, or $10,000.

You also don't have to buy the most expensive newsletter. You'll see in our evaluation that there are high-quality newsletters that charge as little as $99 a year, and they often run specials that can reduce this price.

Believe it or not, our government really seems to want us to invest in companies by buying stock. Although it is not the intention of this book to discuss tax strategy, it is worth noting that there may be tax advantages for certain income levels at this time.

For anyone who doesn't think that they have the funds to invest, consider the following:

> *If you are buying stocks in an individual retirement account (IRA) and you are a married couple making less than $60,000 per year, you can earn a tax credit equal to 10 percent of your contribution. So, the $1,000 stock purchase*

you just made will not only allow you to lower your taxes by $1,000 (brings your income to $59,000) but by an additional 10 percent or $100.

If your income is less than $36,000, the credit is 50 percent of the contribution. Imagine the benefits your children could reap if they started saving early for their future.[2]

You need to check with your tax adviser if any of these options are relevant for you and/or if they are still available.

The only other consideration you need to make before you get started is…

What Kind of Investor Will You Be?

Before you ever start investing on your own or with a financial adviser, you must answer this very important question. You really need to figure this out because it will determine what you buy and sell. If you don't go it on your own, it will allow you and your adviser to be on the same page. Your adviser can't make a plan and know how to implement it without this information.

Who Are You?

- *Investor?*

  This is someone who is long-term oriented and doesn't let market ups and downs get in the way of his or her ultimate goal.

- *Trader?*

  This is someone who tends to be short-term oriented and looks to capitalize on market moves.

- ***Speculator?***

  This is someone who is extremely short-term oriented and a risk taker looking for large returns. He
  or she must have the stomach for large declines.

  If you are a trader or speculator, this book is not for you!

The other important question you need to ask yourself…

Once I start investing, am I disciplined enough to work with an as-
set-allocation model, or do I need someone to help me with this?

The whole idea behind **asset allocation** is not having all of your eggs
in one basket. Think Enron—the company employees who put all
their money into this one stock lost everything. You need more than
one stock, more than all stocks in the same category (e.g., pharmaceutical stocks), and more than only stocks.

Obviously, if you are starting out with limited funds, you won't have
a mix of stocks, bonds, and so forth, and the point of this book is not
to delve into other options but to remind you that you need to be
diversified.

> **Asset allocation:** *Diversifying your investments so that you
> don't have all your eggs in one basket.*

Somewhere along the line you may be wondering why a non-invest-
ment professional, like myself, would write a book about investing.
Because I think anyone can become an investor given the right tools.

## CHAPTER 2

My Journey to Now

"Simple can be harder than complex: You have to work hard to get your thinking clean to make it simple. But it's worth it in the end." —*Steve Jobs*

My Story

When I started investing, I had a great "go-to" source of information, my father-in-law. He used a stockbroker back when that was the only way to buy stocks. He also liked to do his own research and provide input to his broker. For that, he used financial newsletters.

My father-in-law believed in stocks. He liked to read about businesses and what they were doing and talk about new discoveries and why they were going to make a company successful and make him money. He didn't believe in mutual funds—too many fees. This man was a child of the Depression (the big one in the 1930s), and he knew how to bargain and get the most value out of anything. Best of all, he and my mother-in-law used to talk about their investments and had a grand time comparing notes. That's what my husband and I do now, and people always wonder how a couple that has been married forever has so much to talk about. Ah, an added benefit of being investors.

Anyway, back to my story.

I enjoyed talking to my father-in-law about companies and what they were doing because I was running a company at the time. We were a public company (sold stock), and I was the vice president of one of the divisions. As such, I was responsible for tracking profit and loss and all the other aspects of our manufacturing division. However, in talking to him, I soon realized that there was a big difference between what I (or the other division managers) did and what made our stock fluctuate. We could be having a great year, and our stock wouldn't do much of anything. The reverse could also be true.

My company provided a subscription to the *Wall Street Journal*, and I was a faithful reader. But the investor and stock jargon often confused me, and the opinions were all over the map. Never mind that it couldn't give me any direction in what was a "good" stock and what wasn't. So, I decided to follow my father-in-law's advice and subscribe to his favorite newsletter. He assured me that the authors of the newsletter really seemed to know what they were doing. Being in my thirties at the time, I wasn't about to take an older person's advice as sacrosanct. So, while I subscribed to the newsletter, I wasn't about to put hard-earned money into its recommendations. At least, not yet!

Instead, I set up a "dummy" portfolio (list of stocks I thought I would buy) with the newsletter's recommendations that met my requirements in terms of price, dividends, and so forth. I also randomly subscribed to two other newsletters, set up their dummy portfolios, and let them "slug it out."

I was doing this back when it meant going through the *Wall Street Journal* Stock Charts and using a notebook and then, finally, an Excel spreadsheet. With today's technology, following stocks is a click away.

I thought I would give them six months to see if I would have made money had I actually purchased them.

During those six months, I did some homework, and I found out about the strategy of the writers and a lot about businesses that were unfamiliar to me. Best of all, I was really enjoying this little contest.

When the time was up, my father-in-law's recommendation had indeed come out on top. That portfolio showed the most instances of stock-price increases. (I guess there's something to be said for someone who's been there, done that.)

After I started my newsletter subscriptions, I was inundated with "free" publications, most of which were little more than advertisements from publishers. I must say they do a very effective job of reeling you in and making you believe they are not ads. Anyway, I read them all at first and found that I was learning a lot about the jargon of the market and whom I believed and who was "just in love with himself." Yes, most of those were men.

However, many years later, and after some wrong moves (an investment in Flea Fare, a company that had just gone public and provided franchises to flea markets—are you kidding me?—yes, we lost all our money), we started to get it right.

And we have pretty much gotten it right ever since. And it wasn't that hard.

But it took a long time to learn. I want to show you how the learning curve can be shortened for you.

There's my reason for writing this book. Investing isn't only for professionals; it's also for average guys or girls who know what they want (e.g., a new home, a second home, a comfortable retirement), have the discipline to follow a couple of rules, and enjoy what they're doing.

Are you in?

Sonja's Criteria for Investing

The first thing you will need to do is decide what rules you want your stocks to meet. When I started, mine were as follows:

1. **It had to pay a dividend.**

   If I was going to give the company my money, I wanted something for it, regardless of whether the stock was going up or down.

2. **It had to be below $50 per share in cost.**

   We were young and poor. This was a lot of money.

3. **It couldn't be a retail stock.**

   Restaurants and retail stores were out for me—because of rapidly changing trends, these companies make me nervous. But that's just me.

4. **The advantages of owning the company had to outweigh the disadvantages.**

    I determined this according to a checklist I developed. (I'll share this with you later.)

Except for the price of stocks, my original criteria haven't changed much.

Now, I guess you want to know how I've done. Well, my husband and I are retired—and way before any official retirement age. We are doing what we love…keeping track of our investments, traveling, and enjoying our life together. I'm writing, something I have always wanted to do, and my husband is playing the flute (think Jethro Tull or The Moody Blues) as much as he can with his band and at our church.

So, if you're willing to save, work a decent job whose reward may be neutral or positive, read a financial newsletter once a month, and follow some guidelines, you could have a similar end result.

Stock investing is all about *making* money, not losing it. That may sound trite, but I have heard many an investor rely on his or her knowledge of a certain market to pick stocks. Then there's the investor who is always after the hottest stocks even after they have reached their highs. This does not take into account the many variables that determine where single stocks or whole industries are headed.

First and foremost, don't try to go it alone. The stock market is full of trends, hearsay, calculations, and formulations that make up the predictions for what will happen to a stock or industry. You can't possibly research them all, but knowing where to go to get the information you need and trusting that information is what will ultimately help you succeed.

What Not to Do

DON'T go to the TV. These folks are in the entertainment business, not the moneymaking business, except for themselves. They need to scare you, show off their knowledge, or make you laugh. None of these will make you money!

DON'T decide to buy the stocks solely in your area of expertise. Just because you are a realtor doesn't mean that realty companies or homebuilders are good stock buys.

DON'T go to the next happy hour and expect to pick up some good stock tips from a friend or business associate. If that person is such a great stock picker, why isn't he or she retired or out on his or her yacht?

DON'T feel the need to jump into the next great initial public offering (IPO). (Remember the Flea Fare fiasco.) For one thing, you probably won't be able to get any shares, but there is a whole "science" on how to invest in IPOs. Don't gamble with your money because, in essence, that is what you would be doing.

IPO stands for initial public offering. An initial public offering is the first time that the stock of a private company is offered to the public.

Basically, don't listen to anyone who doesn't have a lot of sources and isn't tuned into the market.

DON'T try to go through long-winded books that give you more information than you probably need to know but don't help you make an educated decision.

When I started, I wanted the best possible formula to achieve my goal. To me, that meant following good advice and doing what had helped others succeed. And I wanted proof. I also had an additional caveat. **If I was going to invest in a stock, I wanted to be paid for it. I almost always buy a stock because it pays a dividend.** It may take months or even years for the stock to go up, but with a dividend, I know I will get money back once a year, at least, for owning the stock.

I knew when I started that I didn't have the time or inclination to make this a full-time study project. So, thanks to my father-in-law, I found a better alternative: the financial newsletter. Fortunately for me, he was using one that had already worked out well for him, so I could simply do what he was doing. But he didn't share his investing results with me, and I wanted my own proof, so I started investigating financial newsletters.

What to Do

DO set up a list of criteria for your investments, such as only dividend-paying stocks, stocks of industries in your comfort range, or stocks with realistic investment costs, for example.

DO invest in a couple of financial newsletters that have a good track record.

## CHAPTER 3

Where Do You Fit In?

"No one is truly free who is a slave to his job, his creditors, his circumstances or his overhead." —Alexander Green, Chief Investment Strategist, The Oxford Club

Millenials
If you're a millennial (born between 1981 and 2000) or as I like to say, someone who has a long time horizon ahead of them...

How do you get started and why should you get started?

If you are entering college or just graduated, you may have been fortunate enough to get some monetary gifts. Here's what can happen with those gifts.

We'll look at a recent graduate we will call Judy. She's nineteen, has been out of high school for a year and has a part-time job. She is smart and takes her graduation money, adds a little savings to it (she's living at home and able to save), and puts away $2000 into dividend paying stocks. When the dividends are paid out, she's smart enough to let the dividends buy more stock.

A year later, Judy gets her dream job and starts to invest in the company's 401(k) and totally forgets her initial stock purchase. As she gets closer to retirement she decides to check that forgotten investment and she's surprised to find she has SEVEN MILLION DOLLARS! You will see how this could happen in a later chapter.

If you are fortunate enough to have the benefit of a 401(k) or similar plan at work, and especially if there is a match by your company, use this as your first choice for investing. Once that's maxed out and you continue to get raises, you might want to take some part, or all of those raises, and do some investing on your own.

Then, as with anything you do in life, have a plan! If you're going to go back for an advanced degree, you will probably consider all the possibilities and then decide how best to proceed in terms of commitments (job, family, leisure time, etc.). You need to do the same when you start investing.

Maybe you'll be like our fictional Judy and buy one stock that your newsletter recommends and re-invest the dividends and let it ride. You may still read continuing issues of the newsletter that found you that stock, but because you don't have the time, you'll scan the issues and learn about the market as you go along.

Maybe you'll find the newsletter issues so interesting that you look forward to each one. You may decide to keep buying more stocks. Here is where the time factor comes into play. If you're comfortable with one stock you plan to hold for a long time, you won't have a big-time commitment. If, however, you decide that you want to become more involved, then you'll have to set aside more time.

The best analogy I can think of is, if you like to cook. You will spend time finding the right ingredients, prepping them and doing the work because of the satisfaction you get from the results.

I happen to think investing provides the same results. The monetary rewards give you:

- freedom to travel, and learn about other cultures.
- ability to give your children the best possible education without having them mired in debt.
- ability to give to causes that matter to you.

OK, so now I've told you how I think you can make more money, but you're not convinced the stock market is the way to go. After all, isn't that where your parents lost a lot in 2008?

> *Was it because the media scared them out of their stocks,*
> *and they sold at the bottom of the market?*

I'm not here to trash the media (really, I'm not), but they are not the place to get investment advice.

Here's the real deal: if these parents were invested in quality dividend paying stocks, whatever they lost on paper would more than likely have been regained in the years afterward. I know we are wired to push the panic button, but this is also the reason many investors lose money. The money invested in the market should be able to stay put for at least three years. Don't use funds that you need for everyday living.

But back to what happened. In October of 2007, the S&P (Standard and Poor's 500 of the largest stocks) fell 57 percent. Let's say your parents were invested in some of those stocks and let's say they lost that much. I can relate. Ours went down 35 percent. Better, but still scary.

What did we do? We said, "it will come back." By 2013 the S&P had recovered. Yes, that's over five years but this is invested money, not money needed for everyday necessities.

Now, here's the real kicker, some of those stocks were ones that <u>increased</u> their dividend during that horrible time. For me, that's the sign of a strong company. My re-investment gave me more shares which in turn gave me more dividends.

By buying companies that increase dividends, you do well even when the stock market is going down. This is where compounding comes in which I'll comment on in later chapters and show you the calculations later in the book.

Unfortunately, many people sold right into the panic. Even if you never do anything recommended in this book, I hope you remember that!

Generation X

If you're part of Generation X (born between 1965 and 1981) you're probably well on your way to retirement and college cost goals. If not, the beauty of your situation is that you have 30 plus years until retirement. If you didn't start putting some money into a 529 plan for your kids when they were born, start now. If you want to do this on your own, choosing dividend paying stocks and reinvesting the dividends should pay off big time in college funds.

As far as retirement and the effects of the 2008 recession, refer to the paragraphs above. The right dividend stocks will get you well on your way to adding to retirement income.

Baby Boomers

What if you're a baby boomer (you know who you are) and think it's too late to start investing…

If you have at least ten years during which you can put away some money, there are dividend paying stock techniques that will work for you. One of the newsletters that I recommend has some terrific ways to play catch-up with high yield vehicles. Once again, it's quality newsletters that can help you get started. Later in the book I'll show you how to find them.

There's another reason the baby boomer generation needs to understand investing; you don't want your grandchildren or nieces and nephews to be riddled with college debt. Teach them about money and they will respect it and learn to understand what it means in their life (besides the latest technology) and give them a sense of security.

What if, whenever you give them money, they used a portion to buy whatever they wanted and another portion to invest? When they're little, how about some shares of Disney stock? What products do they use/like? How about shares of Colgate-Palmolive? (You know them for Bounty, Crest, Gillette).

I am throwing out names that are easily recognizable. In the case of Colgate, this is a stock that has raised its dividend consistently over the years. A good choice. But, what if a company you select starts to have problems. How will you know? More important, how will you know when to get out?

That's where newsletters come in. They have your back.

Using newsletters to invest is like using a realtor to buy a house.

Realtors are experts who can help you with affordability, information about the school system, taxes, cost of upkeep and any other questions you may have about your potential investment.

So how do you select a stock? You listen to a friend who gives you the latest tip on a technology stock he/she heard about, go with a Jim Cramer pick on TV because he screamed BOOYAH about a stock so it must be good, or just like the sound of a company name. If you think I'm kidding about these reasons, think again.

If you subscribe to a newsletter, you now have a "realtor" in the investment business. Usually every month or so they will give you a stock pick based on…wait for it…..ACTUAL RESEARCH! Wow, what a concept.

So, if you plan to start investing on your own, that's my piece of advice. You need a newsletter to give you the research to make an informed decision about what to buy and when to sell.

A newsletter is your starting point in picking a stock. You won't have to learn jargon, rely on hearsay, or a TV show. The writers will have checked the market for the best stock with the best potential for making your investment grow.

## CHAPTER 4

Getting to Know Justin & Judy: Why You'll Love Compounding

"Compounding is the greatest force in the universe"
— Albert Einstein

Why Would You Want to Know About Compounding?

BECAUSE IT SETS YOUR INVESTMENTS ON AUTO-PILOT!
Find the right stocks, leave them alone, and you're good to go.

Yes, it's easy if you **pick the right stocks! A newsletter will make this decision easy!**

Remember Judy in the introduction? She made one investment when she was young and it was worth enough to give her a seven million-dollar retirement without doing another thing. That's compounding. She had lots of time (forty-six years) and used a dividend paying stock that increased its dividend payout each year.

Those are the **two requirements for compounding to work best-time and dividend paying stocks.**

Judy had a friend named Justin.

Let's Meet Justin

Justin is a little older, twenty-six, when he decides to start investing. He's got the same $2000 that Judy started with but his timeframe is forty years. He also doesn't add to his investment. Fortunately, he's smart enough to invest in dividend paying stocks and he re-invests the dividends. By the time, he's sixty-six he will have almost one million dollars. Not bad, but not as good as Judy because of the time factor. (You will find the assumptions and calculations in an upcoming chapter).

Now we know that compounding works best the more time you have!

Let's Look At Some Other Possible Situations.

Situation #1

Let's assume that you bought a stock last year and you have ten years in which to have compounding work for you. Let's stay with an initial investment of under $3000.

Maybe you bought two-hundred shares of this stock we'll call NICE for $14.077 ($2815.40). The stock paid you a dividend of $0.15/share or $30, four times last year. That's $120. You told your broker or financial adviser that you want to reinvest the dividends from now on. That $120 bought 8.52 shares. So now instead of getting $30 four times a year, you are getting \$31.28 per quarter or \$125.12 a year. Plus, the price of the stock may have also gone up.

> **Dividend:** *A dividend is a payment made out by the company to its investors. This is often in cash but can be shares of stock. It usually comes from the earnings of a company.*

For those of you with this ten-year time span, let's assume that the dividend is increased every year during those ten years, by seven percent and let's assume the stock goes up two percent. In ten years, you will have almost \$4000. Your \$2815.40 turned in a 42 percent increase and you have almost 30 more shares of stock. Can you get that with a CD or bank savings account? Doesn't this make you want to look for other stocks with this potential?

Situation #2
With a relatively brief time span of ten years you may have more than \$3000 to invest, so let's take an investment of \$10,000. We'll buy 1000 shares of a \$10 stock. We'll assume that you get a 4 percent dividend on your stock and your dividend grows 10 percent per year. In 10 years, you have doubled your money to \$21,000 and you have 700 more shares. If you can wait 20 years it gets a lot more interesting. You could now have over \$80,000 and more than 5000 shares.

Are You Starting To Like Compounding?

> **Compounding:** *Interest paid on both the principal and on accrued interest. This definition is from the dictionary. I like to say it's the generation of monies from continuous re-investment.*

It's Never Too Little or Too Late to Start!

Let's say you want to start investing and taking advantage of compounding. You decide to put $200 a month into dividend paying stocks. You will do that for the next forty years. (During the last two hundred years, a diversified portfolio of common stocks with dividends reinvested has yielded ten percent.)[3] Someone who started at the age of twenty-five would have $1,233,660.60 when they're sixty-five. You can do this calculation for yourself very easily with the calculators I show you later in the book. I'll bet you can't wait to get there.

Doesn't this make you want to start putting away that $200 for yourself, your child or grandchild?

Where will I get the money?

- Do what Judy and Justin did-take monies from gifts.
- Use your tax refund.
- Sell things on eBay or Craig's list that you don't need.
- Examine your budget for luxuries.
- Learn to cook instead of eating out all the time.

Remember our story from Marc Lichtenfeld and how well his eight-year-old daughter could do if she kept re-investing her money? She let her $10,000 investment grow by reinvesting all the dividends and ended up with an annual income from her investments that would take care of her for a long time.

That's the beauty of compounding.

Granted you may not have forty years, and parts of his scenario won't or don't work for you, but it does show the power of money left alone to grow.

What is even more fascinating about compounding is the ability of your investment to grow even if the stocks you own are flat (never really go up or not very much) or go down.

Check out Marc Lichtenfeld's terrific book, "Get Rich with Dividends" which goes into detail on how you can make money with dividends in all kinds of markets.

## Chapter 5

FAQs

"When your outgo exceeds your income, your upkeep becomes your downfall." —Rick Rule

I've told you a bit about myself and how I've been successful with stocks. Also, I've mentioned why you should consider doing what I did and given time and compounding, how you can be successful.

But at this point you may be wondering where do you begin? You may also have some preconceived notions that I haven't brought up.

So here goes….

Frequently Asked Questions

How will my investment in stocks fit in to my overall financial goals?

It can be a small part. If you're like Justin or Judy, you may buy one stock and be done with it.

Or, it can become a bigger part over time. You may decide you like investing, and start to add stocks, and develop a portfolio. For the purposes of this book, we are looking at your personal investing as part of your overall investments, which include ETFs (exchange traded funds), REITS (Real Estate Investment Trusts), bonds, mutual funds, and maybe even precious metals or art. Below is what an overall asset allocation model might look like, from The Oxford Club.

Figure 5.1[4]

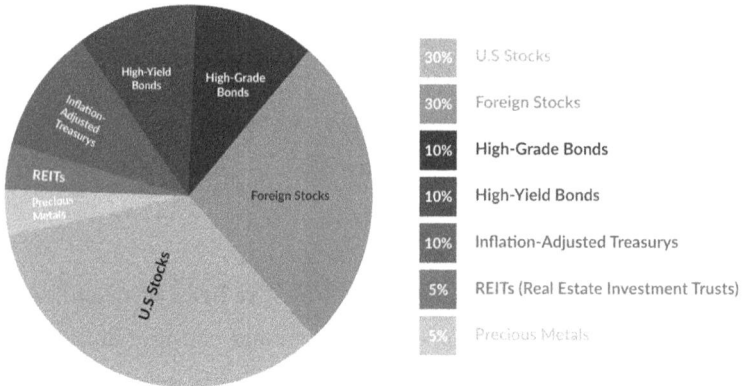

30%	U.S Stocks
30%	Foreign Stocks
10%	High-Grade Bonds
10%	High-Yield Bonds
10%	Inflation-Adjusted Treasurys
5%	REITs (Real Estate Investment Trusts)
5%	Precious Metals

Why haven't you asked me about my risk tolerance?

Every financial adviser will ask you about "risk." I haven't mentioned it yet. I will, but not in the sense that a financial Adviser would ask. He's interested in your overall picture. Here we are discussing a portion of your investments.

Your first risk mediator is your newsletter. If they're worth anything they will let you know when to get out of a stock by sending you a text or email message. This will lessen considerably, the size of any potential loss. More important, I'll show you a tool that will let you determine how much you can bear to lose; and, if you use it, and not let emotion get in the way, minimize any potential losses.

Our other risk moderator is something called a "trailing stop." Later in the book we'll do some calculations. For now, here's how it works:

You buy 100 shares of a stock for $10. You paid $1000.

You decide that you cannot afford to lose more than 25 percent ($2.50 per share) or $250 of that $1000.

You set up a trailing stop, should your stock go down 25 percent to $7.50 you sell it. During the time you hold onto the stock it may go up and down. Let's say it goes up to $15. As the stock has been going up you have been adjusting your trailing stop. At $15 your 25 percent trailing stop is $11.25. What do you do if it goes down to $11.25? You sell it.

You now made $1.25 on each share or $125.

You can only lose the amount you are comfortable with, or make money.

Nice, right?

One stock, one item to keep tabs on. Easy, right?

If you decide to buy more stocks you may want to set up a spreadsheet or use a function called "Trade Stops" that will do the trailing stops for you and even keep tabs on them. The website is tradestops.com.

Just remember, if you're just starting out, a spreadsheet is cheaper. Plus, it's only a couple of computer strokes.

Why can't I just buy stocks in a managed mutual fund and be done with it?

Here are my 2 cents...

Back in the 1980's this would have been the thing to do. Steve McDonald, the Bond Strategist of the Oxford Club says he remembers funds charging 0.7 to 0.8 percent. Today two to three percent is not uncommon. In real terms, if you have a portfolio of $250,000, 0.8% is $2000. Two percent is $5000 or more than double that! In his article, Steve goes on to remind us that 90 percent of the mutual fund managers don't beat the indexes.

There are many articles that corroborate this.[5]

I know what you're going to say, "I have mutual funds in my 401(k) and they're doing well." If you are lucky enough to be doing well, that's great. No doubt it also helps that many companies are matching funds that go into the 401(k) and you can't beat that. However, I would suggest that if you can switch these mutual funds to ETFs you will save a lot on fees.

> *Definition of Exchange Traded Funds: A basket of stocks, usually within a certain industry or index.*

We have some mutual funds and ETFs as part of our overall investments. We watch them very closely and so far, the few we have are doing well. We have been moving away from managed mutual funds into ETFs.

Here is why mutual funds are not the way to go for your personal investing:

1. They are expensive. In most cases, you will either pay an up-front fee or backend fee. One reduces the amount of money you are investing, the other takes the profit and puts it in the fund company's pocket, Then, there are the expense ratios and various marketing fees. Try asking your financial Adviser how much you are paying in fees and odds are he can't tell you the exact amount. It's too complicated!

2. This chart shows how poorly they perform. "...roughly 90% of all U.S. equity funds underperformed their market indexes over a multi-year period. Investors had a 1-in-10 chance of picking a winning fund."

Explanation of the chart[6]

Lagging Behind
Percentage of U.S. equity funds outperformed by benchmark

Fund category Comparison index	Five-Year	10-Year	15-Year
Large Cap S&P 500	88%	85%	92%
Midcap S&P MidCap 400	90%	96%	95%
Small Cap S&P SmallCap 600	97%	96%	93%

*Note: Data as of Dec. 31, 2016
Source: The Wall Street Journal   www.investmentu.com

Figure 5.2

Fund managers are forced to diversify, sometimes causing them to hold too many stocks that dilutes returns. One reason Warren Buffett has been so successful is that he concentrates on certain stocks and industries.

3. One of the ways fund managers are paid is on the size of their assets (dollars in their fund) not necessarily how well they do. They may get 1-2 percent of your investment. That may leave you with an actual return of 2 percent. Today you may be able to get that with a CD that's insured. Let's take a look at that 2 percent return in real terms. You have a portfolio of $100,000. It compounds (there's that great word again) 10 percent per year for 30 years and you end up with 1.7 million dollars. Take out the 2 percent the mutual fund may have cost you and you're down to $1,000,000. Ouch!

4. Fund managers need to keep their portfolios properly diversified. If they have a successful stock that has over weighted the portfolio, they need to sell some or all of it to bring the mix back into proportion. So, they sell and you get the tax bill. How great is that!?

Let's take a look at the difference between mutual funds and exchange traded funds (ETFs)

	MUTUAL FUNDS	EXCHANGE TRADED FUNDS (ETFs)
Definition	A mutual fund is a collection of stocks, bonds, or other securities purchased by a group of investors and managed by a professional investment company. Can be an index fund.	An ETF, or exchange traded fund, is a marketable security that tracks an index, a commodity, bonds or a basket of assets like an index fund. Trades like a stock on the stock exchange.
Fees	Front end or back end & marketing	Low annual fees
Taxes	If a particular stock has done well but becomes too large of a holding in the fund, the manager must sell. This triggers a gain for which the holder of the fund must pay taxes even if the fund as a whole had a bad year.	You pay taxes when you sell the ETF.
PROS	• Simple to own	• Simple to own • Cheap • Tax efficient • Transparent and more liquid
CONS	• Expensive • High Fees • Inefficient tax wise • Too much diversification	• Dividends are lower than owning individual stocks • May have too large of a position in a few stocks

Figure 5.3

Do I need to learn "Wall Street Terms" to start investing?

No. If you follow my advice and subscribe to a good newsletter, you won't have to master terms and you'll continue to learn about the market as you read more issues.

Why do I need a newsletter?

1. How would you know what to buy? In Chapter Two I told you all the places not to go to get stock information. So where will you go? To your broker or Adviser. Guess what, they charge for that and will more than likely suggest a mutual fund "to make life easier."

2. They provide independent research on stocks. The best ones don't have any conflicting affiliations.

3. They understand trends occurring in the market and provide guidance on where to buy.

4. The best ones tell you when to sell. If you are going it alone, as we're doing with independent investing, we still need guidance but it shouldn't come with conflicts of interest.

Can I Become an Investor if I have to pay off debt?

I am not a financial adviser, but my personal opinion would be to pay off the debt first. Knowing the potential of investing might give you the impetus to reduce your debt quickly.

Can I invest in dividend paying stocks in an IRA?

Yes.

When will you get into the nitty gritty of what we have to do?

Right now. In the next chapter I will outline, in general terms, what we're going to cover and then we will get to work and Invest.

## CHAPTER 6

How to Get Started

"I offer nothing more than simple facts, plain arguments, and common sense." —*Thomas Paine*

As you've probably discovered from reading this book so far, I am not a financial Adviser, broker or any other professional in the investing field. I learned by reading, trial and error, and most of all, my mistakes.

I discovered one of the best sources of information on what stocks to buy comes from reading financial newsletters.

I want to help you find a newsletter or combination of newsletters that work for you so you can become a successful individual investor.

The most important part of this is finding the right newsletter.

Here's what I'll do to point you in the right direction:

- Just like you wouldn't want to buy a diamond ring without knowing that you are getting the right carat, clarity and color, you don't want to follow a newsletter that doesn't have a good success rate. Based upon the "Consumer's Report" of newsletters, you'll be able to find the best.

- Then I'll help you decide which one is right for you.

- Once you've made your choice, we'll do a "test drive," pretending we are invested in one or two of the choices offered, for a period of six months. During that time, we'll follow those stocks as if we owned them and see if we make any money.

REMEMBER – YOU AREN'T LEARNING ANY TERMINOLOGY, CALCULATNG ANY FINANCIAL EQUATIONS, and so on. YOU ARE ONLY PRETENDING TO BUY THE NEWSLETTER RECOMMENDATIONS. This is how you'll get a feel for how they work and if they work for you.

- If you decide to "buy" more than one stock, I'll show you how to set up a portfolio.

- Once the test period is over and you decide to buy a stock with real money, I'll show you how to select the right one for you.

- Now you're ready to do the actual purchase through a variety of venues. We'll go over those to see which is best suited for you.

- Simplicity is the beauty of working with newsletters when making your investment decisions.

- Of course once you've started investing you'll want to know how you're doing and if the newsletter you selected is the right choice for you. We'll cover some ways to evaluate your situation.

- We'll look at ways to drown out the noise that comes with investing; advertising you will get now that you're considered an investor.

- You are also probably wondering how a financial Adviser fits into your personal investments.

- I hope you'll also want to know how to have fun with your investments.

Like Thomas Paine's quote at the beginning of this chapter, I want to give you simple, plain arguments and common sense information on why and how you can do this investing thing.

Section One: Invest

Section One: Invest

In this section, we will get into the specifics of investing.

Our fictional investors, Justin and Judy, are different ages and have slightly different timeframes in their investing lives. In the upcoming chapters, we will follow their progress during their investing and reinvesting years.

We will use the DIVIDEND REINVESTMENT CALCULATOR on the next page from the website wealthyretirement.com.

At the end of this section we will have shown their progress in years five, ten, twenty, twenty-five and thirty. You already know how good things get in forty plus years. This will show you what happens in the interim and how time affects your goals.

You can use this calculator to see the possible potential with your particular investments.

Dividend Reinvestment Calculator

Initial Number of Shares:

Initial Price per Share:

$

Annual Dividend:

$

Dividend Annual Growth Rate: %

Stock Price Annual Growth Rate: %

Number of Years:

Dividends Per Year: 1   ▼

Calculator Results

	Without Dividend Reinvestment	With Dividend Reinvestment
Total Value:		
Number of Shares:		
Dividends Paid:		
Annualized Return:		

Figure 1.1

## CHAPTER 7

Finding the Right Newsletter for You

"It's far better to buy a wonderful company at a fair price than a fair company at a wonderful price." —Warren Buffet

What Is a Financial Newsletter?

A **financial newsletter** is a publication (hard copy or online or both) that does independent research on stocks, bonds, and other investment instruments.

For our purposes, we will only be talking about stock newsletters. Most of the writers are former analysts, some of whom became disillusioned with how stocks are sold to the small investor. In my opinion, the best newsletters are those that are not affiliated with any larger organization, don't accept advertising, and don't try to sell you what they advocate.

You can Google "financial newsletters" and come up with thousands of publications, then go through a long and tedious process to find one that matches what you're looking for, *or* you can go right to the industry-trusted source based on my experience and research findings.

This trusted source of information is called "The Honor Roll" and is part of "The Hulbert Financial Digest," HFD for short, written and edited by Mark Hulbert. Mark Hulbert is part of "Market Watch," which is part of the *Wall Street Journal* organization. Mark evaluates around two hundred financial newsletters a year.

Once a year, in December, Mark publishes his list of "The Newsletter Honor Roll." I consider this the *Consumer Reports* of top newsletters because they have to prove their value in good and bad markets to make the list.

Specifically, Mark writes, "To make it onto the HFD's Newsletter Honor Roll, a newsletter must exhibit **above-average performance** in both up and down markets."

Just 15 percent of the almost two hundred newsletters that Mark follows made the list in 2016. I will be updating the list in my newsletter. Be sure to subscribe @**sonjahaggert.com.**

To me, it's even better if newsletters made the list in more than one year. It turns out that my newsletter choice has made the list for fifteen years.

With this list of top newsletters in hand, you can determine your strategy. Following is the 2016 list with some general comments. I favor one particular newsletter because it offers so much more than the others. I do not get any money from this newsletter in sharing my experience or opinion.

Finding Financial Newsletters

The HFD Newsletter Honor Roll 2016[7]

1. Bob Brinker's Marketimer

2. The Buyback Letter

3. Fidelity Investor

4. Investment Quality Trends

5. Investor Advisery Services

6. Morningstar Stock Investor

7. Outstanding Investments

8. The Oxford Club

9. Sound Advice

10. Zack's Premium

Newsletter Honor Roll Review

NEWSLETTER	US MARKET GRADE	DOWN MARKET GRADE	RELATIVE RISK	Since 3/31/2000 EQUITY ANNUALIZED GAIN	TYPE OF INVESTMENTS	STARTED
Bob Brinker's Market Timer	52.1	68.5	75.5	7.30%	US & International equities, fixed income	1986
The Buyback Letter	79.5	75.3	93.3	10.20%	US & international equities	1997
Fidelity Investor	57.5	50.7	83.6	6.30%	US & international fixed income	1999
Investment Quality Trends	75.3	90.4	98.6	10.50%	US & international equities	1966
Investor Advisory Service	84.9	65.8	110.7	10.40%	US & international equities & mutual funds	1973
Morningstar Stock Investor	78.1	67.1	99.9	9.70%	US equities	2000
Outstanding Investments	93.2	52.1	168.8	6.20%	US & international equities	2000
The Oxford Club	61.6	63	87.4	7.60%	US & international equities, fixed income	1995
Sound Advice	83.6	69.9	109.3	9.80%	US & international equities	1993
Zack's Premium	60.3	57.5	102.4	7.00%	US & international equities	1995

Figure 7.1

I eliminated the following from this review: Bob Brinker's Marke-timer and Fidelity Investor. They either do not meet our criteria for investing for the long term (Bob Brinker) or concentrate on fixed income (Fidelity Investor).

Newsletter	TRIAL INFORMATION	INFO @ MAJOR CONTRIBUTOR(S)	YEARLY COST	COMMENTS
The Buyback Letter buybackletter.com			Standard version $195/yr Premium version $79/yr	5 Model portfolios, heavily traded Need to monitor closely Aggressive, trendy
Investment Quality Trends iqtrends.com	$45 for 4 issues	Geraldine Weiss Kelly Wright-mg, editor Michael Minney-publisher Both are also investment advisors	$265 online/yr $310 hard copy/yr other numerous options	First woman to publish advisory service One of oldest newsletters Buy only top dividend paying stocks
Investor Advisory Service investoradvisoryservice.com	Request a sample	Douglas Gerlah editor-in-chief & investment advisor	$215/yr online $259/yr hard copy	3 stock recommendations/ month In depth profiles of companies Economic & market trends in plain English
Morningstar Stock Investor morningstar.com	14-day free trial	Matthew Enffina, editor	$39.95 quarterly $125/yr	Lots of reports & videos In depth reports, ipad version
Outstanding Investments agorafinancial.com		Byron King	$49/yr $62/2 yrs	Emphasis on commodity investments
Oxford Club oxfordclub.com		Alexander Green Chief Investment Strategist	$149/yr	Investment service with many options and fundamental beliefs including long-term investing and minimization of risk. Combine investments with fun & travel.
Sound Advice soundadvice-newsletter.com	4-month free trial		$85/yr $125/2 yrs	No information @ the people giving sound advice.
Zack's Premium zacks.com	30-day free trial		$199/yr	Many options, including trading service.

NB: Bob Brinker's Marketimer and Fidelity Investor are not included because they don't meet our criteria for long-term and/or equity investing.

Figure 7.2

Before you begin to investigate any of the newsletter choices, you need to answer the following questions:

1. What is/are your goal(s)?

   • Retirement

   • New home

   • Second home

   • Nest egg

   • Other

2. How much money do you have to invest?

   • $2,000

   • $5,000

   • $10,000

   • Other

Evaluating Newsletters

How to Find the Right One for You

When writing this book, I made some assumptions about what you wanted out of this book. I assumed that you are new to investing, as well as the following:

1. You don't want to learn all the intricate terms and formulas used by traders.

2. You want guidance on what stocks to buy.

3. You want guidance on when to sell.

4. You want knowledgeable information without conflict of interest.

5. You want to minimize losses.

6. You enjoy making money.

All while not spending a lot of time on your stocks. With that in mind, let's start figuring out what parameters you want to follow.

What limit will you set on the cost of a share of stock?

When my husband and I started, it had to be below $50 a share.

Do you want your stocks to pay a dividend?

In my case, I thought retailers were too volatile, so I avoided them. Maybe you have ethical reasons for not buying certain stocks.

You can add to this list in any way you like, and you can change it if and when your circumstances change. These parameters are useful in helping to make a decision as to whether you will buy your newsletter's latest recommendation.

Plan to purchase one hundred shares at a time. Anything less than one hundred shares is considered an "odd lot." An odd lot will ultimately cost you more money. More on that later.

With these questions answered and the mind-set of at least one hundred shares, you are ready to look at newsletter choices and see what trial subscriptions you want to get.

Once you get your sample issue(s), you will develop a mock portfolio on Yahoo or Morningstar to apply the advice you are getting from the newsletter. I'll show you how to do it in the next chapter.

I suggest following the trial for about six months along with your mock portfolio. This is enough time to watch the recommendations, see the movement of the stock, and get comfortable with your investments and the process.

It is important to follow the newsletter recommendations as if you are actually buying the stock. At the end of six months or so, you will see a pattern develop. Perhaps you selected two or three newsletters and now see that one outshines the other. Maybe you'll select that one to buy and follow.

> *Remember one thing: no newsletter is right 100 percent of the time.*

The newsletters' standings update annually based on features, performance, and other market factors. I update this and other information on my website, **sonjahaggert.com.** Please go there and sign up for the latest information. Yes, it's *free.*

In the next chapter, we'll do a test-drive before we actually plunge into buying our first stock.

Let's check in on Justin & Judy's progress after five years

Dividend Reinvestment Calculator

Initial Number of Shares:	200
Initial Price per Share:	
	$ 10.00
Annual Dividend:	
	$ 0.50
Dividend Annual Growth Rate:	7 %
Stock Price Annual Growth Rate:	2.2 %
Number of Years:	5
Dividends Per Year:	2 ▼

Calculator Results

	Without Dividend Reinvestment	With Dividend Reinvestment
Total Value:	$2,804.97	$2,915.30
Number of Shares:	200.00	261.47
Dividends Paid:	$575.07	$652.27
Annualized Return:	7.00%	7.83%

Figure 7.3

After five years, they have an annualized return of 7.83%. They are doing well but definitely need more time for their money to really grow. Reinvesting dividends is not a "get rich quick" scheme.

Justin & Judy

In Five Years

Without dividend reinvestment	With dividend reinvestment
Value: $2804.97	$2915.30
# of shares: 200	261.47
Annualized return: 7%	7.83%

## CHAPTER 8

Test Drive

*"Investing without research is like playing
stud poker and never looking at the cards."*
— *Peter Lynch, One Up on Wall Street*

It's time to select stocks from the chosen newsletters to see how they perform.

But we are not actually buying anything yet! We are going to pretend to buy stocks by putting them into a sample portfolio and monitoring their progress for a period of time, aka our "test-drive."

When I set up my sample **portfolio**, I had the following parameters I wanted those stocks to meet:

Sonja's Sample Portfolio

1. Must pay a dividend

2. Less than $50 per stock

3. No retail stocks (personal choice because of the rapidly changing trends)

4. Clear advantages to buying

I use checklists I devised to point out advantages and disadvantages of a stock. If advantages outweighed disadvantages, I would probably buy the stock if I could afford it. These checklists can be found in the "Notes and Resources" section of this book, along with a full explanation of how they work.

Portfolio: A group of stocks that you watch and/or own.

What are your parameters? Do you want only dividend-paying stocks? How much are you willing to spend on a share of stock? Are there any stocks you don't feel comfortable buying? Revisit your answers.

Your list may be short, but it will evolve as you go along.

Now that you've had a chance to evaluate several financial newsletters and decided which ones resonate with you, let's pretend you are going to buy some of their picks. The keyword here is *pretend*. You are not spending any of your hard-earned money yet.

As you select recommendations from up to three newsletters, you will put them in your portfolio as if you bought one hundred shares of a stock at the price on that given day. Online websites such as morningstar.com and marketwatch.com let you set up a portfolio and even get alerts. I would ignore this feature because it will be time-consuming.

I used Morningstar in my example to set up our test-drive portfolio and Yahoo Finance to get information on our stock picks because the finance section of Yahoo! is easier to navigate. On Yahoo!, you will find information on those stock picks, such as price today, dividend, and so forth. See the accompanying screenshot of the Finance page of Yahoo!. (This is the way it looks as I am writing this book. It changes from time to time but generally contains the same information.) You will want to start by going to the box marked "Quote Lookup." Put in the **ticker symbol** for the stock that you are going to investigate.

Ticker symbol: the identifying symbol of a stock.

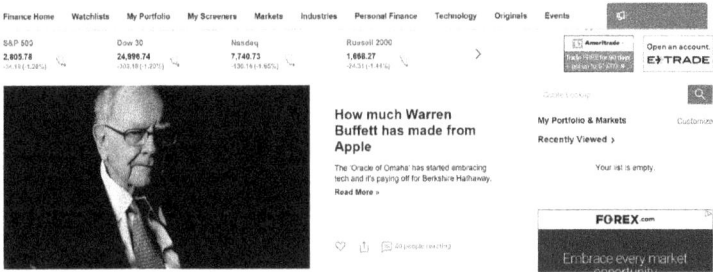

Figure 8.1

In this screenshot you will also see basic market information across the top. There are three main indices listed, the S&P 500, the Dow, and the Nasdaq.[8]

The **S&P 500** comprises the five hundred largest US stocks.

The **Dow** is made up of thirty stocks that are considered a reflection of the US stock market overall. Both are determined by committees at Standard & Poor's.

The **Nasdaq** started as a conglomeration of technology stocks (at the time, growth stocks with less initial capital), primarily because being listed was cheaper, and the entry fee was lower. Today, this index is much more diversified and made up of over 2,500 companies.

These indices are updated continuously throughout the day. Because we are looking at individual stocks, these are *not* an indicator of when we buy or sell.

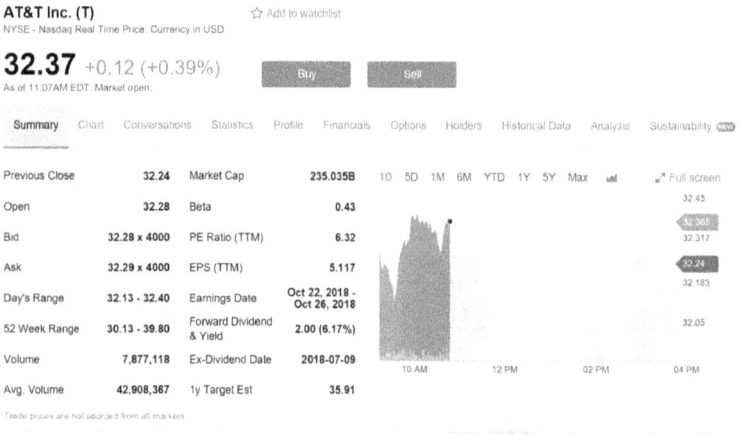

Figure 8.2

What we are concerned with is the box "Quote Lookup." This is where you can put in ticker symbols and find out all about the stocks that you are watching.

When you click "go," it will take you to the stock's summary page. This page will tell you all you need to know to set up or add to a test portfolio.[9]

Keeping Current With Your Stocks

Now that you've set up a test portfolio, you need to decide how often you want to check up on it.

Assuming most of you are not planning to spend every waking moment tracking your stocks, you might want to check your portfolio once a week or every other week. I would plan to do this at the end of the day; the market closes at 4:00 p.m. EST, so I would check around 5:00 p.m. when most of the adjustments have been made. This way, you will know if anything should be bought, sold, held (don't add any more shares), or otherwise noted.

You do need to check the e-mails from your newsletter(s) daily, so I would put an alert on your phone. This will get you familiar with how the newsletter communicates with you and help you not to panic when you actually have real money on the line.

Some of the advisory services will alert you when to sell. Those are the most valuable because recommendations to buy are easy—when to sell, not so much. The latter is worth every penny!

What If You Missed Something?

Here again, I want to remind you that we haven't bought any stock yet.

However, when you do start buying, consider this: Most newsletters will give you some indication of the risk factors associated with their choices. If you buy stocks that pay dividends and let compounding do its job, it's very hard to lose! If you think I'm making a bold statement here, I'll show you what I mean in a later chapter.

Divvying Up the Money In Stocks

How about dividing up your funds?

My favorite newsletter recommends investing only 4 percent of your funds in one stock. That's fine if you have a portfolio, but what if you are just starting with $2,000? That would mean you could only spend $80 (4 percent of $2,000) on a stock. A round lot of one hundred would mean your stock could only cost $0.80. That's a penny stock, and you don't want to go there! Don't ever chase these or let anyone suggest they are a good buy unless you are willing to lose all your money. Think of the movie *The Wolf of Wall Street*.

No Penny Stocks Ever!

No reputable newsletter would recommend penny stocks. We already discussed why, in most instances, you don't want to buy odd lots (less than one hundred shares), so this won't work. I am using one hundred shares at this point to make recordkeeping easy.

I wouldn't recommend waiting around for that "magic" number. What I did was determine the amount of money that felt comfortable for my first purchase. In my case, it was from $10 to $15 a share. Yes, that made the weighting a bit high, but the overall amount didn't scare me. The 4 percent rule comes once you have a real or robust portfolio.

Let's Take a Look at An Example

You start with $2,000 to invest.

You buy one hundred shares of stock A @ $15 = $1,500. That represents 75 percent of your investment capital.

Six months or a year later, you decide to take the $500 you have left from your initial investment and add $500 that *you've saved or gotten as a tax refund and buy another $10 stock. Now your total investment is $2,500, and your initial investment of $1500 represents 60 percent of your total portfolio and the additional $1000 represent 40%. As you keep adding funds or gain more shares from reinvestment, this will bring your allocation down to a comfortable range.*

Of course, as the value of your shares rises, those percentages will change. Your goal, as you keep investing over time and adding to your portfolio, is to bring your investments down to no more than 4 percent for any given stock.

Like many of you, when I started investing, I was busy—in my case, running a manufacturing company and doing a lot of traveling. The information in the newsletter I was reading recommended a stock once a month. However, given that I had my own financial goals and limited resources, I was not going to buy every single recommended stock. I also was not going to buy a huge amount of one stock. Diversification is the key to stock buying—something I will continue to emphasize in this book.

Diversification is the key to stock buying.

Not only do we want to be properly allocated, but we also want to keep in mind that we need to be diversified. Diversification means you will not buy only one category of stock. Even though you may be working in pharmaceuticals, you will not buy only pharmaceutical stocks.

The newsletter you pick will probably have more recommendations than you want to buy or can afford to buy. I have set up two simple checklists that have been helpful in making my decision to buy or not to buy. They can be found at the end of the book. These checklists will be much more meaningful once you have gone through the entire book.

When I first started investing, I wanted to find a workbook (what today would be an online course) that would help me learn about investing. I found that in **The Motley Fool.**

The Motley Fool website, www.fool.com, is a wonderful source of information.

Setting Up a Portfolio

On the following page is a screenshot, Figure 8.3, of what a portfolio in Morningstar would look like.[10] I have used some familiar names for reference only. These are *not* buy recommendations or stock endorsements.

Instructions for Set-Up of Morningstar Portfolio

- Go to Morningstar.com
- Sign In
- Click on "Your Portfolio." If you do not have a Morningstar account, create one.
- Click on "Create New" then continue.
- Enter the stocks you picked.

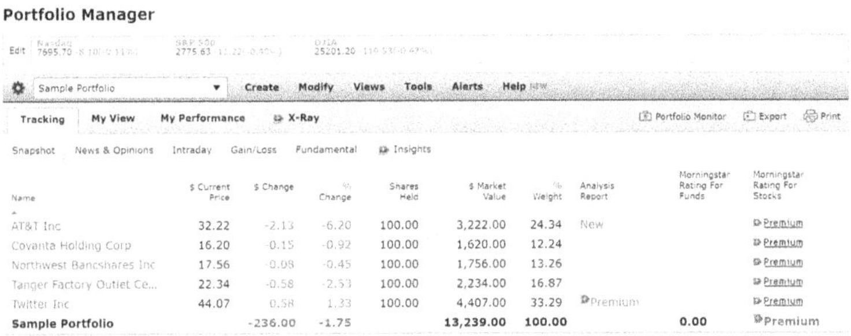

Portfolio Manager

Figure 8.3

Table Column Definitions, For Figure 8.3

- **Name:** We start with the name of the company.

- **$ Current Price:** The dollar value of one share of stock.

- **$ Change:** How much a share of stock went up or down in dollars and cents.

- **% Change:** The percentage change in the price, up or down.

- **Shares Held:** The number of shares you own.

- **$ Market Value:** The total value of each company's shares.

- **% Weight:** How much of the total each stock represents.

DISCLAIMER: This sample portfolio has some well-known names. This is only to help you relate to the fact that stocks are part of our everyday lives. The companies I have chosen for this example are in no particular order and are *not* recommendations, nor do they meet my sample portfolio criteria.

NOW IT'S YOUR TURN TO SET UP YOUR TEST-DRIVE PORTFOLIO

Do so according to the parameters you have chosen and the newsletter picks that fit those parameters. Refer back to the list you made at the end of the last chapter. While you continue reading this book, you will be following your portfolio and probably chomping at the bit to invest some real money. *Don't!*

There will always be another stock that's a winner. Right now, you want to prove to yourself that this newsletter is the right one for you. Remember, it's your hard-earned money, and the whole purpose of investing is *not to lose it*!

Justin and Judy's progress after 10 years.

Dividend Reinvestment Calculator		
Initial Number of Shares:	200	
Initial Price per Share:		
	$ 10.00	
Annual Dividend:		
	$ 0.50	
Dividend Annual Growth Rate:	7	%
Stock Price Annual Growth Rate:	2.2	%
Number of Years:	10	
Dividends Per Year:	2	▾

Calculator Results		
	Without Dividend Reinvestment	**With Dividend Reinvestment**
Total Value:	$3,867.86	$4,548.41
Number of Shares:	200.00	365.89
Dividends Paid:	$1,381.64	$1,888.28
Annualized Return:	6.82%	8.56%

Figure 8.4

Our friends are now up to a 8.56% return and have more than doubled their money.

Justin & Judy

In Ten Years

Without dividend reinvestment	With dividend reinvestment
Value: $3867.86	$4548.41
# of shares: 200	365.89
Annualized return: 6.82%	8.56%

## CHAPTER 9

Figuring Out What to Buy

"A fool with a plan can outsmart a genius with no plan." - T. Boone Pickens

How Do I Decide What to Buy?

You may recall that I said one of the disservices by many who work on Wall Street is to make you think investing is too complicated. Not if you have a plan.

Your plan started when you set up the parameters you wanted your stock choices to meet. Now we take that a step further and add two more considerations: stage of life and asset allocation.

Your Stage of Life

- Am I young enough to take some risks, or am I close to retirement?

- Do I have some money outside of my 401(k) or other retirement account?

If you are young and already saving for retirement through a 401(k) or IRA, you may want to take some cash and invest in small company stocks, which tend to be considered a bit riskier. These smaller stocks may not pay a dividend, but because your newsletter feels they have a great deal of growth potential and could increase substantially in value, they may be worth considering. However, whether you are young or closer to retirement, if you buy dividend stocks and hold for the long term, they will provide the greatest return over time.

If you are closer to retirement, you may want to look at bigger companies, which tend to be less risky.

Asset allocation is all about not having all your eggs in one basket. Once you actually begin buying stocks, you will want to be sure that you have spread your risk among industries, investment types, and parts of the world. The following is what I consider an ideal allocation model from my favorite newsletter.[11]

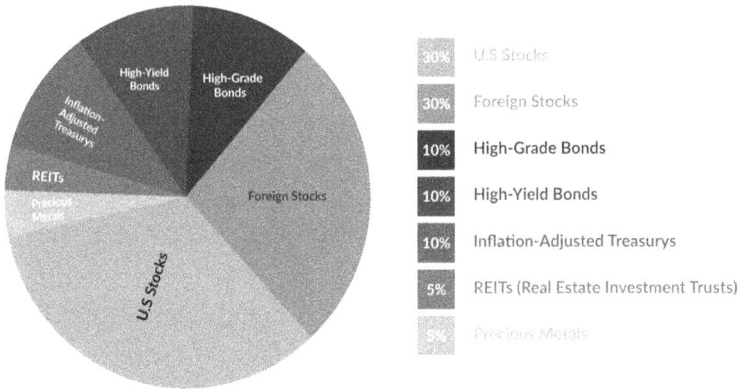

30%	U.S Stocks
30%	Foreign Stocks
10%	High-Grade Bonds
10%	High-Yield Bonds
10%	Inflation-Adjusted Treasurys
5%	REITs (Real Estate Investment Trusts)
5%	Precious Metals

Figure 9.1

Asset Allocation Breakdown

• 30 percent in US stocks

• 30 percent in foreign stocks

• 40 percent in assets such as bonds, real estate investment trust (REITs), and precious metals.

Your 401(k) or other investment vehicle probably has you in some of these assets already. Don't make the mistake of thinking you have to achieve this mix immediately. As you invest, you will get into some foreign stocks. But don't force the issue. Initially, it is more important to start building up your portfolio with some "comfortable" good stocks. Because this book is about stocks, we will concentrate on that.

Here is a **cheat sheet** to reference whenever you are ready to buy.

These reminders will help stop you from getting caught up in the hype that will surround you.

Guidelines to Follow

• **You won't get rich overnight.**

Newsletters are meant to put you on a steady path to wealth, not make you a speculator or gambler.

The best way to make money, especially in the stock market, is to give it time.

You may not want to hear that, but it's been proven over and over again. The theory we are talking about is compounding. Albert Einstein called it "the greatest force in the universe." It has such a major effect on your success in investing that I am devoting an entire chapter to the concept.

• **Don't put all your money into one stock.**

This is true even if it is your company or your father's company. If something goes wrong with one out of ten companies you are invested in, you will only have lost 10 percent, not 100 percent. All those folks who believed that Enron was the greatest company will attest to that.

• **Don't go against the trend.**

Buying a stock as it is going down is not thrifty, it's just plain stupid. If your newsletter is seeing a downward trend, listen and get out.

- **Doubts? Don't do it.**

  You should not buy every stock your newsletter recommends. Make sure it feels right to you. They can't produce 100 percent winners; nobody can.

- **Don't buy only the cheapest stocks.**

  Yes, stick to what you can afford, but it has been proven that the best-performing stocks over the past hundred years cost more than $15. So, if you think that a $5 stock will double faster than a $30 stock, you are probably wrong.

- **Don't buy or sell on emotion.**

  Hopefully, the newsletter you have chosen will guide you on when to buy and, especially, on when to sell.

- **Don't think that being invested in stocks means you are constantly buying and selling.**

  Remember the guideline about compounding. If you have something good, hold on to it!

Keep these guidelines taped to your computer, in your tablet or phone notes, and near any and every device you use to buy or sell a stock. It will save you a lot of anguish.

To drive home the importance of these guidelines, I am putting them on my website for you to bookmark the page and/or print a copy.

Assume that you have gone through six months of the test-drive evaluation and have found the newsletter(s) that you feel are right for you. Hooray!

Now it's time to make that first purchase. How do you go about it? Well, you have four choices when buying stocks.

Buying Stocks

1. **Investment Adviser**

   Contact your investment adviser and let him or her do it. I wouldn't recommend this for the simple fact that an adviser's assistance may cost you up to $100 per stock purchase. You can put that money to work for you in a stock. Plus, why pay for a newsletter if you are going to pay the adviser for this rudimentary task?

2. **Website of Your Adviser**

   Go to the website of your adviser. Some investment companies will let you make a certain number of purchases per month for free. However, check to see the cost of a sale. This may set you back $19.95 or $29.95. Again, this is too expensive in this day and age.

3. **Online Trading Service**

   Check out the many trading services online. At any given time, they may offer specials that make buying stocks very inexpensive. In my checks, I have found many to run around $6.95 or less. Examples of such services include TD Ameritrade and Schwab.

4. **Robinhood App**

   This is a completely free app that lets you buy and sell stock. The company is new, and you will pay some very small fees that the SEC requires; these fees are always passed on to the trader by trading services. The reviews I have read for this app are mixed.

I would recommend option 3 simply because you may need some help as you are starting out. Setting up the account is easy.

At this point, you have made a decision to buy one of the stock recommendations given in your newsletter.

Because you have been watching the news media (only for general news, of course!), you know that market analysts make recommendations all the time about stocks. So, you decide to see what the analysts are saying about your new pick. And, lo and behold, they hate it. *So, what do you do?* You ignore them and listen to your newsletter. *Why?* Without going into any of the gory details of some of their conflicts of interest, game playing, and just being downright wrong a lot of the time, their track record is horrible.

Early in February of 2015 Barron's (a major financial publication) published a study on the track record of the analysts of some of the major firms in the country, including Bank of America, Wedbush, and Stifel. The last two actually lost money.

Buying-and-Selling Game

One last thing. Somewhere along the line, someone got the idea that investing in stocks is all about trading stocks. In order to do that, you have to become familiar with terms and jargon. Then you have to understand formulas, and maybe then you might buy some stock, only to find out that the particular industry is on a downward trend, and everybody hates it. The trend is against you, and you just lost all your money.

Does this happen? Absolutely! But it doesn't have to happen. Hence, hold on to quality stocks that have good fundamentals.

Other investors make different habitual errors. They are too eager to take profits or too reluctant to cut losses. They tend to invest when they feel optimistic and sell when they feel pessimistic. (A great way to buy high and sell low.)

They concentrate their investments in only one sector, such as energy, gold, or technology. Or they put too much money in individual positions. Many investors, for instance, will divide their portfolios among five stocks, putting 20 percent in each. That's not enough diversification, and a single loser can punch a big hole in your portfolio.

In short, you do not have to be constantly buying and selling stock to be in the market and successful.

Purchasing Your First Stock

OK, it's time. Are you ready to buy that first stock and see it take off? Oh no—you just bought your first one hundred shares, and they immediately went down!

Happens all the time. But don't panic. Everything that goes down must come up and vice versa. Plus, you have two safeguards that will keep you from losing more money than you are comfortable with. The first you know already, and the second will be a safeguard so that you don't lose more than you are willing, if any at all:

5. **Listening to your newsletter.**

   If you have a newsletter that tells you when to get out, *do it*! Don't second-guess it; don't think that suddenly you know better. *You don't!*

   After all, the newsletter's authors have spent years studying trends and other influential factors.

6. **Setting up a trailing stop.**

   Second, with all of your stocks, decide how much you are comfortable losing. We will set up a **trailing stop** to make sure we don't lose more than we can handle. This may sound like the worst kind of advice, especially when I've said all along that you should only make money, not lose it, but you will come to appreciate this mechanism for the insurance it can provide.

What we're talking about here is a safeguard because "stuff happens." What we're going to do with all of our stocks is set up a spreadsheet. You can do this the old-fashioned way on paper, or online.

Trailing Stop

We are going to decide ahead of time how much, in the worst-case scenario, you could afford to lose. Let's consider the following situation:

Situation

- *You bought a stock at $10.*

- *Let's say you could lose 15 percent of your money ($1.50) if it went down drastically. Your trailing stop is $8.50.*

- *The next day it went up to $11.*

- *So, you calculate that 15 percent of $11.00 is $1.65 or $9.35 (your trailing stop)*

- *You keep doing this as the stock goes up: 15 percent @ $14.00 = $11.90 (your trailing stop)*

- *You do nothing when the stock goes down.*

Should the stock go down to $9.35 from $11.00, you sell it at a small loss. If it went down to $11.90 from $14.00, you would sell it but would still have made money.

This trailing stop should be part of your Excel spreadsheet portfolio where you follow your stocks. Because you will be checking your portfolio once a week and updating the stock prices, this will be the perfect time to update your trailing stop.

Use the trailing stop, and you will be a better investor than the majority of folks out there!

It's time to check in with our friends again and see where their investments are after 20 years.

Dividend Reinvestment Calculator

Initial Number of Shares:	200
Initial Price per Share:	
	$ 10.00
Annual Dividend:	
	$ 0.50
Dividend Annual Growth Rate:	7 %
Stock Price Annual Growth Rate:	2.2 %
Number of Years:	20
Dividends Per Year:	2 ▼

Calculator Results

	Without Dividend Reinvestment	With Dividend Reinvestment
Total Value:	$7,190.19	$14,582.96
Number of Shares:	200.00	943.69
Dividends Paid:	$4,099.55	$10,111.87
Annualized Return:	6.61%	10.44%

Figure 9.2

Justin and Judy have continued to reinvest their dividends. This is where their accounts would stand if all the parameters we identified from the start had not changed.

Justin & Judy

In 20 Years

Without dividend reinvestment	With dividend reinvestment
Value: $7190.19	$14,582.96
# of shares: 200	943.69
Annualized return: 6.61%	10.44%

## CHAPTER 10

Buying a Stock

*"Buying a stock is easy. Finding the
right one is hard." - Sonja Haggert*

Where you get your stock recommendations is the most important
part of individual investing!

All the research in the world you do on a company doesn't mean
anything if the stock sector is out of favor, or there is a fundamen-
tal problem with their business. Even so, there are stocks that can
overcome a negative trend but you need someone in tune with the
market to dig out the details.

We are letting our newsletter choice(s) do the digging for us. Now
that we've seen a number of newsletter issues, did a test drive, and
feel comfortable enough to buy our first stock, here's how we do it.

- Go to the recent issue of your selected newsletter and decide if this stock is one you want to buy based on the criteria you set up (cost, dividend, and so on).

- If you decide you will buy, figure out how much money you can afford and if you can purchase at least 100 shares.

- Pick your favorite online platform (i.e. TDAmeritrade, Schwab, E*trade) set up an account, and buy the stock.

- Set up a trailing stop. This will help make sure you don't lose more than you can handle. I like to call this "casualty insurance." Here's how it works:

  1. You buy 100 shares of a stock for $10.00, spending $1000. You set up a trailing stop (let's say 25 percent) at $7.50 or a limiting loss of $250.

  2. The next day it goes up $1.00 to $11.00 and you "made" $100.

  3. You set a trailing stop at $8.25. {$11.00 X .75 = $8.25}

  4. You decide that you can lose 25 percent or $275 of that $1100 if it goes down.

  5. You do NOTHING if the stock goes down unless it hits $8.25. If that happens, you sell it. This takes the emotion out of the decision to sell. Let's hope most of the time your stock goes UP. As it goes up, you increase your trailing stop.

6. At $15.00 your trailing stop would be $15.00 X .75 = $11.25. In that case, if it goes down to $11.25 and you sell it, you made $1.25 on each share or $125.

I like to throw in a bit of advice here: if a newsletter tells you to get out, DO IT! Don't second guess them; don't suddenly think you know better, YOU DON'T. They have spent their career studying trends and fundamentals. Besides, you are paying for their advice. Use it!

During the course of being invested in a stock, it may go up and down more than my example. You have a discipline in place so that should a company lose a patent fight or introduce a new product that bombs, you will get out before things get ugly.

Your "pass to get out" is your trailing stop which is easy to use, works within the parameters you set up, and keeps you from waiting for things to get better (stock to go back up). Do this and you can pat yourself on the back for being a smart investor.

Justin and Judy are in their 25th year.

Dividend Reinvestment Calculator

Initial Number of Shares:	200
Initial Price per Share:	
	$ 10.00
Annual Dividend:	
	$ 0.50
Dividend Annual Growth Rate:	7 %
Stock Price Annual Growth Rate:	2.2 %
Number of Years:	25
Dividends Per Year:	2 ▼

Calculator Results

	Without Dividend Reinvestment	With Dividend Reinvestment
Total Value:	$9,770.80	$31,396.59
Number of Shares:	200.00	1,822.26
Dividends Paid:	$6,324.90	$24,567.94
Annualized Return:	6.55%	11.64%

Figure 10.1

Now we start to see some more dramatic results. Recall that in five years, their return had doubled. When we last checked in with Justin and Judy at twenty years, they had $14,000. Now that $14,000 has more than doubled.

Justin & Judy

In 25 Years

Without dividend reinvestment	With dividend reinvestment
Value: $9,770.80	$31,396.59
# of shares: 200	1,822.26
Annualized return: 6.55%	11.64%

Section Two: Reinvest

Section Two: Reinvest

We've followed Justin and Judy as they have continued to reinvest. After they have been reinvesting for 30 years the numbers are looking pretty good. In fact, since we left them at year twenty-five, the additional five years have brought their investment to almost $80,000.

Dividend Reinvestment Calculator	
Initial Number of Shares:	200
Initial Price per Share:	$ 10.00
Annual Dividend:	$ 0.50
Dividend Annual Growth Rate:	7 %
Stock Price Annual Growth Rate:	2.2 %
Number of Years:	30
Dividends Per Year:	2 ▼

Calculator Results		
	Without Dividend Reinvestment	With Dividend Reinvestment
Total Value:	$13,288.07	$79,556.09
Number of Shares:	200.00	4,141.39
Dividends Paid:	$9,446.08	$67,174.59
Annualized Return:	6.52%	13.06%

Figure 2.1

Justin & Judy
In 30 Years

Without dividend reinvestment	With dividend reinvestment
Value: $13,288.07	$79,556.09
# of shares: 200	4,141.39
Annualized return: 6.52%	13.06%

## CHAPTER 11

Holding on to
a Good Thing

*"Dividend stocks outperform everything else over
the long haul—and almost certainly will in the future too."
- Dr. Jeremy Siegel, professor of finance at the
Wharton School of the University of Pennsylvania*

Compounding

So far, you've heard a lot in this book about how to invest in stocks to make money. This chapter is about how to set that on autopilot.

Are You...

- *a young mother who wants her child to go to college and not have to pay back loans forever?*

- *just married and know that you will be responsible for your retirement?*

- *a single professional who wants to know you are building security in your life?*

- *a retired couple who want to save for your grandchildren?*

- *a single or married professional who wants a second home someday?*

- *someone who wants a better lifestyle and knows the lottery and crime are not the way to get it?*

Then compounding will become your new BFF.

There are two requirements for compounding to work best: time and dividend paying stocks. We've seen how this has worked for Justin and Judy during a thirty-year time span. Now let's dig into their circumstances a little bit more.

Revisiting Justin & Judy

When we checked in with Justin and Judy they had $80,000. All along we have been using the same timeframe and same parameters for these imaginary folks. They haven't added anything to their initial investment but have continued to reinvest their dividends.

Now our example of time and dividend paying stocks takes a dramatic turn. While Judy will continue to reinvest for another sixteen years for a total of forty-six years, Justin will reinvest for an additional ten years for a total of forty years.

Justin After Forty Years

Here is where we might find Justin's initial investment of $2000 after forty years if the variables we used remain the same.

Dividend Reinvestment Calculator		
Initial Number of Shares:	200	
Initial Price per Share:		
	$ 10.00	
Annual Dividend:		
	$ 0.50	
Dividend Annual Growth Rate:	7	%
Stock Price Annual Growth Rate:	2.2	%
Number of Years:	40	
Dividends Per Year:	2	▼

Calculator Results		
	Without Dividend Reinvestment	With Dividend Reinvestment
Total Value:	$24,739.53	$978,431.42
Number of Shares:	200.00	40,972.70
Dividends Paid:	$19,963.51	$893,835.01
Annualized Return:	6.49%	16.74%

Figure 11.1

What really makes this example so dramatic is the huge increase in the number of shares of stock which significantly increases his income from dividends. Figure 11.1 shows the actual calculation.[12]

Judy After Forty-Six Years

OK, now let's look at Judy. She was nineteen when she decided to take her $2,000 of graduation money and put it into dividend-paying stocks and reinvest the dividends.

She's worked and contributed to her 401(k) and totally forgot about this $2,000. At the end of forty-six years, without depositing another dime and letting her dividends reinvest, and all the variables remaining the same, she has almost eight times what Justin has, with only six additional years. Figure 11.2 shows the value of Judy's one investment of $2,000. All we have done is extended the time frame by six years.

Pretty amazing! In fact, so amazing I couldn't believe the calculations and went to two other sources to verify these results. They all had Judy at eight times wealthier.

Wow, now we have the power of starting early and reinvesting. Odds are you won't hold an investment for this long and the variables we used will change yet it is worth looking at what the future could hold.

Dividend Reinvestment Calculator

Initial Number of Shares:	200
Initial Price per Share:	$ 10.00
Annual Dividend:	$ 0.50
Dividend Annual Growth Rate:	7 %
Stock Price Annual Growth Rate:	2.2 %
Number of Years:	46
Dividends Per Year:	2 ▾

Calculate   **Reset**

Calculator Results

	Without Dividend Reinvestment	With Dividend Reinvestment
Total Value:	$36,117.33	$7,673,261.63
Number of Shares:	200.00	281,993.31
Dividends Paid:	$30,675.18	$7,181,191.04
Annualized Return:	6.49%	19.65%

Figure 11.2

Let's try an example with a well-known company and see what happens.

In order to find the information we need to fill in the blanks in the calculator, we will go back to Yahoo Finance, or you can use the website www.dividendinvestor.com. Both will give you historical data. For our example, we will be using Yahoo Finance.

Let's use AT&T as a familiar example. AT&T is considered a "**divi-dend aristocrat.**" That means that AT&T is an S&P 500 company (large company, considered a relatively conservative investment) that has raised its dividend every year for the last twenty-five years.

On Yahoo Finance, go to the box marked "quote lookup," and en-ter the ticker symbol "T" to find the following information for the AT&T stock.

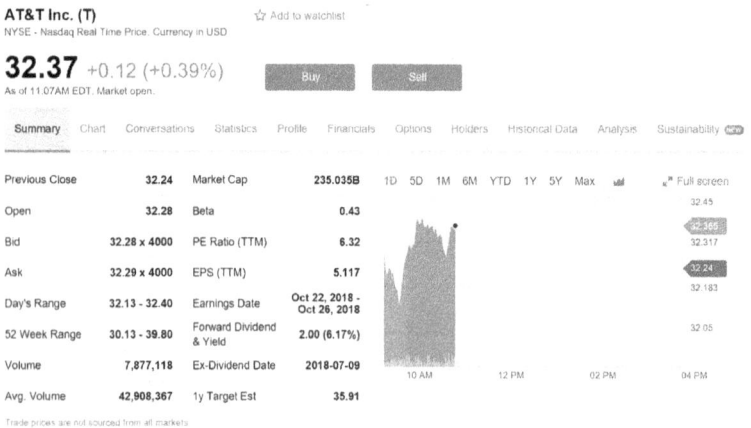

AT&T Inc. (T)
NYSE - Nasdaq Real Time Price. Currency in USD

32.37 +0.12 (+0.39%)
As of 11:07AM EDT. Market open.

Previous Close	32.24	Market Cap	235.035B
Open	32.28	Beta	0.43
Bid	32.28 x 4000	PE Ratio (TTM)	6.32
Ask	32.29 x 4000	EPS (TTM)	5.117
Day's Range	32.13 - 32.40	Earnings Date	Oct 22, 2018 - Oct 26, 2018
52 Week Range	30.13 - 39.80	Forward Dividend & Yield	2.00 (6.17%)
Volume	7,877,118	Ex-Dividend Date	2018-07-09
Avg. Volume	42,908,367	1y Target Est	35.91

Figure 11.3

Now we're going to find the annual dividend. From the Summary page on Yahoo Finance, click on "historical data." Then click on "div-idends only," and then click on "time period" and go to "3yrs." Then hit "apply." You will see that AT&T pays dividends every quarter, and in January of 2017, AT&T raised the dividend to $0.49/share or $1.96 per share. In 2016, it was $0.48 per quarter or $1.92/share, and in 2015, it was $0.47 per quarter or $1.88/share.

For the **Dividend Annual Growth Rate,** we want to put in 2 percent . For this compilation, it looks like AT&T increases its dividend around 2 percent per year.

Date	Dividends
Oct 06, 2017	**0.49** Dividend
Jul 06, 2017	**0.49** Dividend
Apr 06, 2017	**0.49** Dividend
Jan 06, 2017	**0.49** Dividend
Oct 05, 2016	**0.48** Dividend
Jul 06, 2016	**0.48** Dividend
Apr 06, 2016	**0.48** Dividend
Jan 06, 2016	**0.48** Dividend
Oct 07, 2015	**0.47** Dividend
Jul 08, 2015	**0.47** Dividend
Apr 08, 2015	**0.47** Dividend
Jan 07, 2015	**0.47** Dividend

*Close price adjusted for splits.   **Adjusted close price adjusted for both dividends and splits.

Figure 11.4

For the **Stock Price Annual Growth Rate**, we will use the same screen to put in a request for stock prices. AT&T stock prices move around, but even if you have a stock that goes down, don't panic. Remember, a stock that raises its dividend every year means that when you reinvest, you are getting more shares at a bargain price because the stock price went down.

Let's fill in the blanks. When I looked at AT&T for the year 2017 (as I'm writing this), here is what I found.

Date	Open	High	Low	Close*	Adj Close**	Volume
Dec 01, 2017	36.35	39.33	35.81	38.88	37.25	588,631,100
Nov 01, 2017	33.86	36.90	32.55	36.38	34.86	879,382,500
Oct 06, 2017				0.49 Dividend		
Oct 01, 2017	39.20	39.80	33.33	33.65	31.84	821,503,000
Sep 01, 2017	37.59	39.31	35.10	39.17	37.07	563,552,300
Aug 01, 2017	39.25	39.27	37.20	37.46	35.45	407,609,400
Jul 06, 2017				0.49 Dividend		
Jul 01, 2017	37.84	39.67	35.81	39.00	36.43	567,280,000
Jun 01, 2017	38.68	39.37	37.54	37.73	35.25	436,895,300
May 01, 2017	39.68	39.70	37.45	38.53	35.99	467,181,000
Apr 06, 2017				0.49 Dividend		
Apr 01, 2017	41.60	41.77	39.52	39.63	36.58	410,612,000
Mar 01, 2017	41.78	42.70	41.26	41.55	38.36	380,077,200
Feb 01, 2017	42.28	42.46	40.41	41.79	38.58	372,470,500
Jan 06, 2017				0.49 Dividend		
Jan 01, 2017	42.69	43.03	40.24	42.16	38.47	460,517,200
Dec 01, 2016	38.63	42.84	38.16	40.38	36.85	463,518,700
Nov 01, 2016	36.97	39.67	36.10	38.63	35.25	500,059,800

Figure 11.5

Running Numbers

In my calculations, I used the dividend rate in 2017, which had gone up to $0.49 a share quarterly, or $1.96 per year.

Let's say you bought 100 shares of AT&T in December, 2015 at $29.88. In five years, assuming all the parameters have remained the same, you have gone from an investment of $2,988 (100 shares at the $29.88) to 4,895.82.

You've made almost $2,000. And because you chose to reinvest your dividends, your yield is 10.38 percent. Try getting that from the bank. Realize that these numbers are strictly an estimate, but they are based on what could happen.

When it gets really interesting is looking ten and twenty years out to see what your potential return could be. The calculations are on the upcoming pages.

Not bad for essentially doing nothing.

Dividend Reinvestment Calculator

Initial Number of Shares:	100
Initial Price per Share:	$ 29.88
Annual Dividend:	$ 1.96
Dividend Annual Growth Rate:	2 %
Stock Price Annual Growth Rate:	3.7 %
Number of Years:	5
Dividends Per Year:	4 ▼

Calculator Results

	Without Dividend Reinvestment	With Dividend Reinvestment
Total Value:	$4,603.22	$4,895.82
Number of Shares:	100.00	136.63
Dividends Paid:	$1,019.99	$1,193.44
Annualized Return:	9.03%	10.38%

Figure 11.6

Dividend Reinvestment Calculator

Initial Number of Shares:	100
Initial Price per Share:	
	$ 29.88
Annual Dividend:	
	$ 1.96
Dividend Annual Growth Rate:	2 %
Stock Price Annual Growth Rate:	3.7 %
Number of Years:	10
Dividends Per Year:	4 ▾

Calculator Results

	Without Dividend Reinvestment	With Dividend Reinvestment
Total Value:	$6,443.17	$7,827.00
Number of Shares:	100.00	182.15
Dividends Paid:	$2,146.15	$2,971.11
Annualized Return:	7.99%	10.11%

Figure 11.7

Dividend Reinvestment Calculator	
Initial Number of Shares:	100
Initial Price per Share:	$ 29.88
Annual Dividend:	$ 1.96
Dividend Annual Growth Rate:	2 %
Stock Price Annual Growth Rate:	3.7 %
Number of Years:	20
Dividends Per Year:	4 ▼

Calculator Results		
	Without Dividend Reinvestment	With Dividend Reinvestment
Total Value:	$10,941.82	$18,723.42
Number of Shares:	100.00	302.99
Dividends Paid:	$4,762.28	$9,239.40
Annualized Return:	6.71%	9.61%

Figure 11.8

Why I Love Compounding

Compounding is so fantastic that even in weak markets, bear markets, and markets that go nowhere, you can make some real money if you hold on and let those dividend-paying stocks do their work.

Section Three: Rest

At this point Judy can sit back and be pretty comfortable in her retirement. Depending on Justin's other financial resources, he may decide to wait an additional six years to catch up to Judy.

## CHAPTER 12

How Are You Doing?

"Timing the market is a fool's game. But time in the market is your greatest natural advantage." —Nick Murray

How Are You Doing?

At this point, you've invested real money. Now you want to watch what you're doing on a regular basis. My recommendation is once a week. You have established parameters. You have established what it means to be successful. And your newsletter and trailing stops are helping you decide when to sell.

Let's begin by acknowledging that we are not day traders, so don't check your stocks every day. Pick a day of the week when you'll see how you are doing and stick with that strategy. We always look at our stocks on Saturday. The markets are closed on Saturday, and we have all weekend to evaluate our situation.

The easiest way to check your stocks is to use the "stock" app on your phone.

Our KYW Radio in Philadelphia also does periodic reports on the market during the day.

There are, however, special circumstances. We have had days when the market went up drastically or down drastically. On those drastically up days, I hope you have decided when and if you want to take a profit. My father-in-law subscribed to the theory of "let's not get greedy" and sold half his shares when they doubled. That way he, was "playing" with the house money. I have also heard investment professionals say they let a winner ride until it goes down 15 percent or refuses to rise when there is bullish (really good) news. Or you may let them ride along with your newsletter.

Hopefully, you subscribe to a newsletter that has your back when things go downhill—as in, you will get an e-mail recommending that you sell. If you have a trailing stop in place, *it* will also tell you to get out, not your emotions.

We discussed trailing stops in previous chapters, but I think it is such an important concept that it's well worth repeating and explaining in more detail.

Why Trailing Stops Are So Important

A trailing stop is a trigger, which you set, that will tell you when to sell a stock. You can use this independent of the newsletter telling you when to sell or along with it. Here's how it works.

- *You buy a stock for $10 per share.*

- *You decide at what point you will get out if the stock starts to decline. Let's say you could lose 25 percent or $2.50 per share.*

- *You set a trailing stop at $7.50 per share. This means that at the end of a trading day, should your stock hit $7.50 per share, you sell it. No questions asked, no emotion involved.*

- *Odds are, your stock goes up and down during the week. At the end of the week when you check it, let's say it has gone to $10.25 per share.*

- *Now you go back and change your trailing stop to $7.69 per share (25 percent). Now your stock has to go down to $7.69 per share, not $7.50, before you sell it. So, you continue to lose only 25 percent of the highest price your stock hits.*

- *This is a number you can choose, or your newsletter may make a recommendation.*

The trailing stop moves up when the price moves up. Simple, right?

Why use 25 percent? No reason. You may decide to use 10 percent all the time because that is all you would be willing to lose. It's self-discipline. The whole idea is to protect you from seeing a stock go down and down while you continue to think it will go back up, so you do nothing. Psychologists say that's the way our brains are wired, we will do everything to avoid hitting the "sell" button.

Because you have a strategy, this won't happen to you!

OK, at this point, you've bought good stocks and perhaps sold some that went up and sold a few that hit their trailing stops. When you sell with a trailing stop, this is often at a profit from your initial investment; that scenario follows.

Trailing Stop With Profit

- You bought a stock at $10.
- Over time, it has gone up and down. At this point, your trailing stop is at $37.50.
- Your stock has gone up and down.
- Now your stock is at $50.
- The stock starts to go down. You hit the trailing stop of $37.50 and *sell*.
- You *made* $27.50 per share.

You're not waiting around for the stock to go up again because of your discipline.

On days when the market drops drastically, you'll be so glad you have this policy in place. Then, if this is still a good stock (and your newsletter agrees), you can buy back shares at a cheaper price. *Don't you just love a sale?* Well, the stock market has them all the time.

> *So, back to the question at hand:* ***How are you doing?***

Let's evaluate your success by what is called **yield** in the market. This is a really simple equation. Read on even if you hate math.

> **Yield:** *Dividend divided by stock price.*

Example of the Value of a Yield

Here's an example. Your stock pays $1 per share, and right now the stock trades at $50. So, $1/$50 = 0.02. 0.02 x 100%=2 percent. As I'm writing this, we are at a low interest rate, and most banks are paying around or under one percent on deposits. So, that 2 percent looks pretty good. But remember, the beauty of stocks is that you also expect that the price of the stock will rise so that you make out with the dividend and hopefully also with the increased price of the stock.

What I look for are stocks that grow their dividend—once a year if possible.

Let's assume that the stock in the previous example grows its dividend by 10 percent so that the dividend is now $1.10 ($1.00 × 0.10=0.10 and $1.00 + 0.10=$1.10) Dividend growth and stock price tend to have a strong correlation, so the odds are that the price could rise to $55 over time ($1.10/$55) to keep that 2 percent yield. Obviously, this cannot be predicted, but history shows that it does happen.

Another Scenario to Sell Stock

There is another time when you may want to sell a stock. If you've run out of money to make a new stock purchase, get rid of the worst stock in your portfolio. That may be one that doesn't have a dividend and/or hasn't gone up significantly or is stuck in limbo.

Keeping Tabs on Your Stocks

Lastly, make sure that you have a system to track your stocks. A simple Microsoft Excel spreadsheet works for me. Anything will do that works for you and gives you information when you need it.

Although I am a firm believer in watching your stocks and being on top of your trailing stops, there is a strategy you can employ if you feel you're too busy to be diligent.

Before going into the specifics, this strategy calls for a real-life story. I know I said I wouldn't bore you with prose, but this story is worth telling…perhaps some of you even read it in the news. Here is my version paraphrased from a *Washington Post* article.[13]

*A resident of Vermont, Ronald Read, died at the age of ninety-two. His career was comprised of working at the local gas station for twenty-five years, followed by working as a janitor at the local J. C. Penney for seventeen years. The perfect example of someone who was not well connected, not well educated, and not a business owner, he left **an estate of $8 million.***

How did he make his fortune?
In the stock market. Surprisingly, he wasn't the best stock picker. He even owned Lehman Brothers, which went to zero.

So, how did he do so well?
The stocks he bought were conservative, blue-chip stocks of well-known companies whose businesses he understood. (Sound familiar? I think Peter Lynch is famous for a similar strategy…) Examples of his holdings include American Express, Proctor and Gamble, and General Electric. Most important, he reinvested his dividends, and he thought long term. He didn't try to time the market because he knew that doesn't work.

What else did he do right?
He diversified his holdings and spread his risk by owning ninety-five different stocks. In my opinion, that's too many to watch. But then again, he didn't watch them.

He kept his investment costs minimal, and he lived frugally.

The most important takeaway I have from this story is that *you can just let your stocks run without paying too much attention*. Will you do as well? That depends on whether you can "leave well enough alone" when the stocks start to go down—in other words, be in it for the long term. When you reinvest dividends, you have to accept small increases in the short term for big increases after about ten years. You have to live somewhat frugally in the beginning because your first priority is having money to invest.

There have been other examples of people doing well with little attention given to their stock holdings. If you have a long-term strategy (ten or more years) and can handle ups and downs, you probably need to pay less attention if you buy solid dividend-paying stocks and continue to reinvest the dividends.

Fidelity Investments[14] did research on its most profitable accounts and found that they were the ones where people did nothing. That's right - nothing!

There are, however, ways to gauge if the fundamentals of a company are deteriorating. But that's what your newsletter should be doing, so you shouldn't have to deal with that—just make sure you read it. Most newsletters worth their salt will have you move out of a position because they have seen the fundamentals shift and send a sell signal.

Now, let's get to a little math. If you never added anything to your portfolio, determining your return would be simple.

Return on Your Investments:

(Note: This is a simple equation that does not take into account any additional monies that you may add.)

[(Ending portfolio value ÷ beginning portfolio value) – 1] × 100 = your return in percent.

For example, if you ended with $2,700 and started with $2,000, your increase would be 35 percent:

[($2,700 ÷ $2,000) – 1] x 100 = 35%

[(1.35) – 1] x 100

[.35] x 100

= 35%

You may have added to your portfolio during the year, and that is not taken into account in this simple equation. An easy way to account for any changes is to determine in what quarter you added or subtracted a given amount and then go back to this simple equation.

The best and very simple stock-performance equation I have found was written by Jeff Brown of the *Philadelphia Inquirer*.[15] He puts the calculation this way:

> *In stocks, total return is figured by combining the change in the stock's price with any dividends the stock paid. So a stock that went from $10 a share to $12 a share (its price appreciation) and that paid a 50-cent dividend per year, has a total annual return of $2.50 or 25%. Its price appreciation alone was 20%.*

Another favorite writer is Jonathan Clements. He used to write a column entitled "Getting Going"[16] for the *Wall Street Journal*, one of which is extremely valuable for its simplicity. He called it "Confused by Investing? Maybe It's the New Math." The part I especially like is "10 plus 10 equals 21," explained as follows:

> *Imagine you invest $100, which earns 10% this year and 10% next year. How much have you made? $21.00.*
>
> *Here's how the math works.*
>
> **Year One: $100 x 10% =$10**
>
> **Year Two: $110 x 10% = $11**
>
> $10 + $11 = $21

This year's 10 percent gain turns your $100 into $110. The next year, you also earn 10 percent, but you start the year with $110, resulting in an additional $11, boosting your wealth to $121.

That's what compounding is all about!

Ex-Dividend Date

The **ex-dividend date** is a very important factor to keep in mind when selling. However, it should not be the be-all and end-all of when you sell.

> **Ex-dividend date:** *The date on which you must own the stock to get paid the dividend.*

Let's say you own a stock and know you will be getting a dividend on June 1. You go to Yahoo Finance, and it says that the ex-dividend date is May 15. That means that you must own that stock on May

15th, in order to receive the dividend. If you sell it on the 16th, you will still get the dividend. If you sell it on May 14th, you will not get the dividend.

Should it keep you from selling a stock that is going down? In this case, you will have to determine for yourself if the dividend is worth it.

Balancing Your Portfolio

One thing I chose not to discuss in the narrow focus of this book is balancing your entire portfolio. Because we are only talking about one aspect of investing, stocks, I won't go into how you should be diversified in bonds and other investment vehicles—that is a topic for another book down the road. For some of you, that might be why you start a relationship with an investment adviser.

## CHAPTER 13

Don't Believe Everything

"There is no correlation between economic growth and stock prices." - Alexander Green

Why Shouldn't I Believe Those Statistics, Lies, and Myths?

Now that you have subscribed to two or three newsletters, you will find yourself getting a ton of advertising on every conceivable topic that may or may not be related to investing. Suddenly, what the president of Algeria said yesterday will affect your international stocks, what Jim Cramer just said means you probably should sell that oil-industry stock, and one of the financial papers said to load up on Internet stocks. And that's just what you read when you checked your phone on the way to work.

Do me a favor right now: don't listen to any of it! First of all, if you do, you won't have time for anything else. And that's not the point of this book. This book is to make your investing life easier, not harder.

Second of all, one doesn't have anything to do with the other. Investing is about companies, not economic theory, politics, or the media. And lastly and more importantly, you are paying good money to listen to your newsletters, so do it!

Any newsletter worth its money will tell you that the news has little to nothing to do with how your stocks perform. Yes, initially it will look like there's a relationship. If a war breaks out in some part of the world, the stock market will react, but not for long. And in that stretch, if you panicked and sold stock on the way down, you may have lost some serious money.

But don't take my word for it. I'll give you some insights on past performance/history from professionals in the finance field.

Peter Lynch is one of the best-known names in mutual funds. He managed the Fidelity Magellan Fund from 1977 to 1990, during which time it grew to $14 billion. His returns averaged 29 percent annually. He is noted for saying that if he spent thirteen minutes a year thinking about economics, he had wasted ten of those minutes.

Dr. Steve Sjuggerud, a noted financial columnist, said the following in an issue of his newsletter, "Daily Wealth":

> Go ahead and read about all the "macro" stuff—the economy, the Federal Reserve, government policy, tax law, and interest rates. Form your own opinions and ideas. Even debate your views with friends and family.
>
> **Then—and this is the most important part—forget all about your macro views when you find a great business trading at a bargain price.**

Buffett and his business partner Charlie Munger claim to have never discussed the economy once in nearly 50 years together. They just buy bargains.

Most investors do exactly the opposite. They read all about the president…GDP growth…and government debt…and they get scared out of buying great businesses at bargain prices.

The other danger with listening to pundits is their advice often involves predictions. Often, those predictions are wrong. But have you noticed how they are rarely taken to task because the readers have moved on? The following discussion includes a sampling of just a few of the recent predictions from some very credible sources.

In 2013, John Hussman, who writes for the website Business Insider, predicted the possibility of a 40 percent crash in the market.[17] At the time when he wrote this, in November of 2013, the S&P 500 was up more than 20 percent. The year ended with all the market indices (Dow, S&P 500, and Nasdaq) up in the double digits. The Dow was up 26.5 percent, the S&P 500 was up 29.6 percent, and it was a banner year for the Nasdaq, up 38 percent. I recall reading somewhere that these gloom-and-doom predictors keep saying the same thing until it happens. In the meantime, you could have made some real money.

Remember the "Great Recession" that started in 2008? The S&P 500 (that's made up of the largest stocks) lost 37 percent of its value that year. By the end of 2013, it was up well over 90 percent! Imagine if you had listened to the media, which, in this time of panic, said, "Sell, sell, sell."

In a *Forbes* post in June of 2014, there is a quote by John Bogle of Vanguard Mutual Funds.[18] In April of 2013, Bogle predicted that "the stock market would decline by 25-50 percent in the coming decade." He cited the typical maxim that basically says, "Everything that goes up must come down," noting that the market had gone up for an inordinately long time. But where does he get the percentages? Of course, the magazine goes on to agree with him by citing all kinds of economic factors. Even if this happens, let me refer you back to the paragraph before this.

My favorite prediction and one that had me laughing out loud was in a July 28, 2014, posting on the CNN Money site.[19] They asked three psychics to make market predictions. My reaction: *Really?* Anyway, my favorite was by Thomas John, a medium and clairvoyant in New York City. This quote is from that post: "He said he took 20 minutes to light a candle and do some meditation before firing off an email to CNN Money with his predictions." The other two were even weirder.

As if that isn't bad enough for the average and/or new investor, then we also have the dramatic posts. Early in 2017, the Money section of the USA Today site ran with a headline that said, "Stock Plunge Digs Deeper."[20] The Dow only fell 2.2 percent. With the Dow hovering over 17,000, that was hardly a major decline. But the media loves to use scare tactics so that you will continue to read and/or listen in. They want you coming back, and scare tactics work really well.

I could share many more instances of trying to rationalize a fit between economic policy and the stock market, but I think you get my point. There is no correlation. What you will be getting from your newsletters is recommendations for good stocks of quality companies with a bright future that have good earnings (making good profits). And as I've heard from just about anyone who follows the market, **stock prices follow earnings**.

But just for the fun of it, let's put a few more statistics, lies, and myths to bed.

Wall Street has some clichés that are worth noting because they will come up in the literature you read from time to time. Here are the ones you'll probably hear most often.

Wall Street Cliches

"Santa Claus Rally"
At this time of year, people tend to look for brighter days, and profits are usually strongest during the fourth quarter.

"As goes January, so goes the year."
In January of 2016, the Dow Jones Industrial Average had the worst beginning to a year ever!

Does that mean we should sell everything? The really terrible month ended down about 5 percent. What's important to note is that this adage has been right, but only 87 percent of the time since 1950. So, if you have quality stocks that pay a dividend, do you really want to dump them? Probably not.

"Sell in May and go away."
From May through September, the market has historically risen less than during the winter months.

"Summer Rally"

I'm not sure I understand this one, as summer tends to be the weakest time for the stock market. Usually, there is at least one rally, but who knows when that will happen.

"Beware the dead cat bounce."

This refers to the saying, "Even a dead cat will bounce a little." In the stock market, that means a short-lived rally or upturn in the market. Couldn't they think of a better phrase?

Are you going to sell all your shares of stock in May? Are you going to buy as many shares of stock as possible in December? I doubt it. So, the next time some Wall Street guru mentions one of these clichés, you know what to do—ignore it! Just imagine how much you would pay out in buy/sell fees by following these clichés!

Bull and Bear Markets

These terms refer to the up (bull) and down (bear) markets that happen on a regular basis.

A **bear market** starts when the market is down 20 percent. It's important to remember that with the Dow hovering around 22,000(as I'm writing this), when it goes down 200 (less than one percent) or 300 (1.4 percent) points in a day, that isn't so traumatic in percentages. We're not talking close to double digits here, like during the 2008 and 2009 downturn.

Bear markets have historically lasted eighteen months. The right attitude says we take this as a sale and buy those stocks we have wanted but were too expensive.

Bull markets last about eight years (yes, years) on average. That's a lot longer than a bear market, but the latter gets all the attention.

During especially turbulent times, like in 2008/2009, the S&P 500 lost more than 30 percent of its value. As scary as that was, the S&P 500 was up more than 90 percent by 2013.

This has also happened to other indexes, and if you are willing to look at the "real" numbers, you won't scare as easily and will look at the numbers for what they mean, not what someone has scared you into believing.

Now to the most important part of this chapter. Have all the financial experts and even some of the newsletter editors convinced you that the stock market is too complicated and that you can't do this? I hope not. Because you have a wealth of research you just did behind your decisions. You are listening to top-ranked newsletters with the guys and gals who do a lot of research and have given you the facts to make buying decisions that fit the criteria you defined.

You are going to shut out all the media noise when it comes to your investing decisions.

## CHAPTER 14

Advisers – Need vs. Want

*"Only those who want everything done
for them are bored." - Billy Graham*

*"Wall Street is the only place that people ride
to in a Rolls-Royce to get advice from those
who take the subway." - Warren Buffet*

Do You Need/Want An Investment Adviser?

If that isn't a loaded question!

Before I go on, you may be wondering why I chose to use two quotes to start this chapter. Maybe you didn't notice, but I want to tell you why.

With regard to Billy Graham's quote, I think people should understand what is being done with their money. After all, didn't you work hard for it?

The second quote from Warren Buffet relates to my general feeling about investment advisers. Do I want them driving around in a Rolls-Royce and spending their weekends on a seventy-foot yacht? No way! That probably means they are charging me way too much money. On the other hand, do I want them to look like they desperately need to replace that 1970 Toyota? No way! That means they may not know what they're doing.

We are creatures of perception, and that perception is often important. It certainly is when you're picking an investment adviser.

What I'll aim to do is help you find someone who "feels" right in some important ways. It's obvious why some people need advisers from the get-go:

- They are too busy.
- They are emotional when it comes to their money.
- They don't understand financial concepts and have no interest in learning about them.

If these reasons don't apply to you, you might still want to consider an investment adviser. Ask yourself these simple questions:

- Is everything I do always right?
- With whom would I rather bounce off ideas—a neighbor or someone who is familiar with investments?
- Am I going to want to establish a relationship with someone when I'm eighty, or should I do it now when there's time to get to know someone whom I hope to respect and trust?

- Do I have a plan, and most important, do I always stick to it?
- Do I always keep emotion out of my investments?

I think we've established pretty well that there should be someone in your life to be a partner in your financial endeavors. As I've said throughout this book, the best first source is your newsletters. You've taken the time to get to know their philosophies, they have hopefully made you some money (if not, you need to find new ones), and they probably have e-mail or other avenues available to ask questions.

But when it comes down to helping with tax questions, your individual situation, or the "what would you do in my boat" types of questions, they can't be specific. That's for your tax accountant/certified public accountant (CPA). So, I would say just about everyone needs a person to go to for the "warm and fuzzy" questions. Plus, I am realistic enough to admit that when I'm in my eighties or nineties, I may not want any part of managing my portfolio.

Now I'm not saying that is going to be easy. But as you're starting out, there's no rush to get it done, either.

If you are just starting to invest, many advisers have a minimum dollar amount you must invest in order to work with them. This can be waived if that adviser feels you are committed to saving. Actually, that's fine—this will give you time to build up your portfolio and do the investigation to find a suitable adviser. There's no rush to get it done.

If you already have a portfolio (an absolute minimum starting amount is probably $100,000, but it is most often $500,000), then you have a wider range of choices.

Let's start this discussion with some job descriptions of those who work in the financial industry.

First, there's the **stockbroker**. I'm sticking my neck out here, but I don't think many even exist anymore with the advent of E*TRADE, Schwab, and others that let you buy and sell stocks to your heart's content, often for what you would pay for a cup of coffee. Well, these days, your trade may be cheaper than that cup of coffee. Those that are left provide advice for a fee and buy and sell for you.

You already get the advice from your newsletter, and you can buy and sell online by yourself. So, unless you have never touched a computer and can't do your own buying and selling online, this is one person you do not need.

If after reading this book you decide you would like to get involved in buying stocks, a **financial adviser** will help you put together an overall financial plan. And yes, everyone needs a plan. Hopefully, this book has convinced you that you need to be in control of the plan along with the person advising you.

A financial adviser, like a doctor, should have some accreditation. Here are some of the titles a financial adviser may have after his or her name to indicate that he or she has the experience to provide you with advice.

Designation Cheat Sheet

ChFC: Chartered Financial Consultant

ChFCs must complete an educational program given by The American College. This entails investments, financial planning, and insurance. They must also meet experience and ethical standards. Biannually, they must complete thirty hours of continuing education.

CFP: Certified Financial Planner

This is probably the most well-known of the titles. The Certified Financial Planner Board of Standards awards this to candidates who complete their curriculum, pass a ten-hour examination over two days, and show that they have experience with financial planning.

CRPC: Chartered Retirement Planning Counselor

This designation is awarded by the College of Financial Planning to those who complete their study program and pass a multiple-choice test. This designation must be renewed every two years by completing sixteen hours of continuing education and paying a fee.

CEBS: Certified Employee Benefit Specialist

The International Foundation and the University of Pennsylvania Wharton School cosponsor this designation. The purpose of this designation is to show that the individual understands employee benefits and compensation. It requires the completion of eight courses.

CFA: Chartered Financial Analyst

The CFA Institute awards this designation to those who complete a three-year, three-exam course of study in portfolio management and investment analysis. Most of these folks work with institutional investors (think your 401[k] plan).

CPA: Certified Public Accountant

CPAs are required to get a bachelor's degree in business administration, finance, or accounting. They are also required to complete 150 hours of education and have no less than two years of public accounting experience. CPAs must pass a certification exam, and certification requirements vary by state. Additionally, they must complete a specific number of continuing hours of education yearly. This is from Investopedia.[21]

RIA: Registered Investment Adviser

This is a next step after any of the previously described designations similar to a master's or doctorate degree. These folks are registered with the SEC and their state securities regulator.

I'm not sure that having three designations versus one after a name means these financial advisers are smarter or better. Maybe they like to study more or value the titles. At least one is absolutely necessary, though! Bottom line: you need to feel comfortable with the adviser, and after a period of time, the adviser needs to prove to you that he or she has *your* interests at the forefront and *listens* to you. Hint: If your adviser only wants to speak to your husband or significant other, it's a **big red flag**!

OK, so how do you choose? You may be shocked at how we came to work with our adviser. We got credit-card points. But, in our defense, it was a large and respected institution. These days that gives you confidence, not just in the fact that there is a large institution having some control over the adviser's actions but also that there is a healthy amount of identity-theft protection in place.

Most important, we started slowly. We only gave him a small amount of money to work with and vetted him on a number of issues. We let the relationship develop over time and checked him out on sec.gov/investor to see if there had been any regulatory issues. I would recommend that you do this regularly. Remember, this is your money, and trust should only go so far. When you put money into a bank, you know it is insured by the Federal Deposit Insurance Corporation (FDIC) for up to $250,000. You don't have this insurance with a financial adviser.

What about those yummy lunches and sumptuous dinners you get invited to that may pressure you into signing with someone? Go and enjoy the food and the information you get that may be helpful. But understand that this is a form of marketing. These events cost money, and they are paid for by the folks who work with this individual. However, anyone in business needs to market. If you feel this person is someone you would like to work with, check out the adviser's credentials, and start slowly with a small amount of money. Let the adviser prove to you what he or she can do.

So why, if you have a newsletter to guide you in making investment decisions, should you consider an adviser?

First and foremost, you need to make sure that your portfolio is adequately balanced. To be invested only in stocks, (worse yet, one stock), when you have a sizeable portfolio, (such as $500,000) is the worst thing you can do. It will be the adviser's job to see that you are diversified into other investment vehicles so that when the stock market has a rough ride, you are doing well in bonds, REITs, or other investment areas.

Your financial adviser should keep you grounded when the stock market is having a bad run. Hopefully, he or she will tell you that when the market is going down is not the time to sell if you are invested in quality stocks and, better yet, getting a dividend. If the adviser is worth his or her salt, the adviser should appreciate your intel from your newsletter, not fight it. Your trailing stops and the newsletters will be providing details on these stocks that may indeed need to go.

Someday when you're older and may find yourself in a compromised health situation, someone still has to look after your investments. Will you have someone you can trust?

I want to share with you my red flags that you might find helpful as you choose and work with an adviser.

Red Flags With an Adviser

1. For couples, beware if the adviser only wants to talk to one of you. It's usually the husband because he "understands financial information better than women," right? *Wrong!*

2. The adviser says he or she will charge you a percentage to work with you and will make all the decisions. *Not!*

You need to have a discussion, but the adviser must be willing and able to explain all decisions and to consider your input. *Again, this is your money.*

3. The adviser only contacts you once a year to say that everything is fine. *Really?* You should be getting periodic updates with actual data/numbers.

4. The adviser is constantly making changes to your portfolio. Why? Is it to make money through buying and selling?

5. The adviser won't tell you how he or she is paid. ***Very big red flag here!***

If you decide to have your financial adviser invest in mutual funds for you, the last point may be difficult because there are so many fees. Know that before going in. These fees may be hard to decipher, even for your adviser. Work on it, and make sure the increase in your portfolio more than covers the costs. Best of all, stay away from mutual funds and go to **exchange-traded funds (ETFs)**, which have much smaller and better-defined fees. But do remember that you get what you pay for… a financial adviser has to make a living.

My best advice here is this: find a partner. And if things don't work out, be prepared to find someone else. It's your money, and you worked hard for it.

So, now that you've familiarized yourself with this stock investment "thing" and are feeling comfortable and capable, you deserve to enjoy your newfound success.

## CHAPTER 15

Are We Having Fun Yet?

*"We have enjoyed and learned so much
on the pretext of investing." - Sonja Haggert*

You **Can** Have Fun Being an Investor

Did you know that our government actually encourages us to enjoy our investments?

Let me explain.

Become an active investor, and you can travel the world, learn about new advances in technology, and come to understand the importance of solar and wind power—which impact our environment—all while getting a tax break.

When my husband and I first started investing, we knew there were financial seminars we wanted to attend. It just so happened that some of those seminars were in nice places, like Florida, California, the French wine country, and so on. So, we started going. And because that was the basis of our trip, we were able to deduct many of our expenses as a tax write-off. These seminars helped us understand more about our investments, provided a forum to ask questions, and gave us a lot to talk about over dinner. Since tax laws have recently been updated be sure to ask your CPA if you can get any deductions.

We also started attending annual investor meetings for some of the stocks we held. Those events are required by the government, and if you are an investor, you can attend. These meetings gave us a look at the personalities behind the companies and the opportunity to hear them tell their stories.

Imagine going to an annual Apple meeting. Well, you can! Tim Cook was recently on the TV program *60 Minutes*. Own a share of Apple stock, and you can see him in person.

Maybe you just bought a Ford car. Suppose you decided to own some of Ford's stock. If you attend Ford's annual meeting, you will hear firsthand from the CEO and learn why the company is so successful.

The opposite is also true. Perhaps the meeting gives you the feeling that things are not going as well as expected. Perhaps your newsletter is confident things will turn around. Maybe at the meeting, you will learn why. It will also give you the opportunity to question corporate leaders.

Last year, we attended the Bristol-Myers Squibb annual meeting. We received such a welcome that it made us feel really good about being one of the company's investors.

We also attended the Colgate-Palmolive meeting, which was huge and akin to a lovefest because the attendees seemed so happy with their results.

If you're in any way into learning, this can be great fun. You hear the company results first—and not from a third party!

Some common sense is in order here—if you have $1,000 invested in the stock market, I wouldn't suggest that you splurge on a seminar costing $10,000 in some exotic location. You probably wouldn't be able to take advantage of the whole amount anyway. But I'm not an accountant, nor do I pretend to know the tax code, so you need to check with your tax adviser.

Just know that this benefit is out there for you, and learn how to use it to your advantage if possible.

So, where will you go next? How will you enjoy making money? You may want to start by attending the annual meeting of your first stock investment. Or you might want to attend a seminar to learn more about your newsletter's philosophy in investing. The options are endless.

If you subscribe to my blog, you'll get my reviews of the annual meetings we attend, any information we get on upcoming seminars, and notes about some of the interesting people we meet along the way. For example, Marc Lichtenfeld of the Oxford Club is a boxing announcer @stocksnboxing. Marc Lichtenfeld is the Chief Income Strategist at the Oxford Club. I was fortunate to meet him at one of the Club's retreats, after following his investment philosophy through his "Oxford Income Letter." His twitter feed describes him as "author of 'Get Rich with Dividends' and the only published stock analyst to announce world championship boxing and MMA (Mixed Martial Arts)."

Over time, you'll have that sense of accomplishment from making money, playing with calculations that show you what you can achieve, and enjoying the travel that comes as an added perk. If nothing else, you'll be in a better place because you will have an understanding of the financial landscape and your own investments.

MAKING MONEY WITH STOCKS IS AS EASY AS: INVEST with the right newsletter, REINVEST and let your money make more money and REST and enjoy what you have accomplished.

Conclusion

You did it!

You learned how to **invest** without a course, and without reading a lot of books.

Now you'll put what you learned on auto-pilot and **reinvest.**

You'll **rest** and enjoy the benefits of what you have accomplished.

I'm so excited for you. I knew you could do it!

It wasn't hard because you:

- Had the right people (newsletters) to guide you.
- Put discipline into place.
- Know that time will do its job.

I also hope you will discover that this is an avenue to learn about the topics that interest you and benefit by making money from your knowledge. To us, money has meant freedom. Because we are comfortable financially, we have a lot less stress, we can come and go as we please, we can take better care of ourselves, and best of all, we can be more generous with those we love.

Thanks to the newsletters I read, I knew before it became common knowledge that, as a nation, we are winning our battle to become oil independent. I also continue to find out about new advances in the treatment of cancer and other diseases because innovative companies are behind these discoveries, and some might present good investment opportunities.

Thanks to a newsletter, we were able to pass on to our nieces' information about an online bank that offers much better rates on checking accounts.

Speaking of young people, if you have one takeaway from this entire book, it should be that the earlier you get started, the better you will do. So, start talking to your children and grandchildren about money and investing. The sooner they learn that $1,000 today can turn into hundreds of thousands later, the better off they will be. Not only that, but the more secure they will feel.

If nothing else, I hope you become somewhat familiar with the terminology and, best of all, are able to talk with and question your adviser. This will help to establish rapport and respect and cause you to be taken more seriously.

In the next section, I have included my checklists for stocks. Because different sectors of business do things differently, this is not a be-all and end-all, but it is something to use, along with your newsletters, to help you make a decision on whether or not to purchase a particular stock.

These checklists were derived from a wonderful book by David and Tom Gardner, the brains behind The Motley Fool website, entitled *The Motley Fool Investment Workbook*. If you want to understand more of the fundamentals of the market, this is a great source of information. If you really want to understand the fundamentals behind a stock, this book is a great place to start.

Following the checklists is a glossary of terms used in the checklists and an explanation of how to get to those numbers—these break down the components of the checklists and equations.

I have not included a glossary of general terms because it is so easy to find definitions online.

Lastly, I hope you will sign up for my blog at **SonjaHaggert.com** and tune into updates and information on what I have discussed in this book. I do reviews of annual meetings and things you should know to make your first annual meeting comfortable, give book reviews, and provide information on people you should know—and every once in a while, I add something I call "Funny Friday" (you can use your imagination on this one).

Thanks for taking the time to read this book. I'd love to hear from you! Let me know what you think on the blog or contact me through my website.

Notes and Resources

"There seems to be some perverse human characteristic that likes to make easy things difficult." - Warren Buffett

Most readers won't look at this section, and you actually don't need to. You'll have guidance from your newsletters, and you'll learn along the way as you read their commentary.

But maybe at some point, you'll want to add some of your own evaluation to the mix. In my case, I knew enough financial terms to be "dangerous." So, I developed a couple of checklists that either reinforced what the newsletters said or made me cautious, prompting me to decide not to buy that particular recommendation.

In this section, you will find the checklists I devised to help me make a decision.

Sometimes I go with the conclusion; sometimes I don't. These checklists do not work for all kinds of stocks, and they shouldn't be used on their own. As I've said throughout this book, don't just pick a stock because you're an expert in the field, or you like the sound of the name, or it's the latest trend. You're smart enough to go with the experts in your newsletters.

The Checklists

My checklists are broken down according to the market cap (short for capitalization) of a stock. Market cap is the value of a company based on its stock price.

The first checklist is for small to midcap stocks. They are defined as less than $1 billion (small cap) to $7 billion (mid cap) respectively. So, for example, if a company's stock is $10 today, and the company has 10 million shares on the market, that company's market cap would be $100 million. Today, that is considered a small cap company.

Because these companies are small, we expect the good ones to be on a growth trajectory. We look for certain elements that would indicate they are a good buy. The Motley Fool calls these "rule-breaker stocks," and I have used that term to make up my small-cap checklist. On the following pages are examples of how I might evaluate a small cap stock. (Information in checklists is fictional data for example only.)

Checklist #1

		Plus	Minus	NOTES
Stock Name:	ABC Company			
Symbol:	AB			
Market Cap of 500 million to 7 billion	1.27 Billion			
Source:	ABC newsletter			
Business/Emphasis:	printing services			
Price Today:	$18.13			
Share price > $7.00	yes			
Beta in comfort zone (around 1.00)	1.6		-	
P/E (12 or less is cheap)	14.33		-	I like to buy economical stocks so this is too expensive
PEG (1.00 or less is cheap)	3.53		-	again, too expensive for me
Net Profit Margin of 10% or more (net income/sales)	8%		-	89,000,000/11,009,000=8%
Sales growth of more than 25%	-2%		-	sales growth is negative
Earnings growth of more than 25%	N/A			no information available
Positive cash flow (yes or no)	yes	+		
52-week stock price low to high (not at high)	14.79-24.64	+		wouldn't be buying at a new high
50 week moving average above 200 day moving average	no		-	indication is down, not up
Insider holdings >10% but < 50%	N/A			no information
Dividend (yes or no)	yes	+		
Dividend amount 3% or more is great	3.09%	+		
Payout ratio= <75%	240.26%		-	bad indicator that there is not enough cash to pay the dividend
		4	6	Based upon these totals I would not be inclined to buy this stock.

Of course, there are plenty of stocks that are valued at more than $7 billion, and for those, I use the "Rule-Maker Checklist" which you see below.

Checklist #2

		Plus	Minus	NOTES
Stock Name	XYZ Company			
Symbol	Z			
Market cap of > 7 billion	256.33 Billion			
Source	ABC newsletter			
Business/Emphasis	Telecommunications			
Price Today	$41.77			
P/E (12 or < is cheap)	19.89		-	Too expensive for me to buy @ this point.
PEG (1.00 or less is cheap)	1.7		-	Too expensive
ROE (18 or > is great)	10.76%		-	how effectively the company uses its resources. Not so hot.
Beta in comfort zone (around 1.00)	0.39	+		not much volatility-I like that
50 day moving average is above 200 day moving average	yes	+		the trend is up
52-week stock price (lo to hi, not at high)	$36.10-41.35		-	I get nervous buying at a high
Sales growth > 10%	-0.7		-	
Net profit margin of 10% or > (net income/sales)	7.90%		-	12,980,000,000/163,790,000,000
Gross margin >50% (gross income/gross sales)	53%	+		86,900,000,000/163,790,000,000
Current ratio > or = 2:1	0.76		-	
Cash King Margin > 10% (free cash flow/sales)	24%	+		
Dividend (yes or no)	yes	+		
Dividend amount 3% or more is great	yes	+		
Payout ratio <75%	91.9		-	
Foolish Flow Ratio=<1.25				
current assets-cash/current liabilities-short term debt	0.8	+		
(efficient use of capital) found in balance sheet				
		7	8	

Because these are larger companies that, by virtue of their size, cannot be as nimble as the smaller ones, we look at a different set of parameters to evaluate them. Again, I am using the term *rule-maker stock* from The Motley Fool because it is so descriptive.

There are blank checklists included for you at the end of this section.

How Do I Use the Checklists?

Once I have filled in all the information from Yahoo Finance (using the Summary, Statistics, and Balance Sheet pages), I will look at the pluses and minuses for that stock. If there are more pluses, I will lean toward buying the stock. The opposite is also true—if there are more minuses than pluses, I will hesitate to buy the stock. If, however, the newsletter has made a good case, I may go with the newsletter's opinion and buy some shares.

In the case of the preceding examples, I would probably not buy the rule-breaker stock, but I might buy the rule-maker stock when the price comes down—unless my newsletter thinks that this stock is positioned for even more growth.

As you can see, even the numbers on these checklists don't make this a cut and dry decision. So, listen to your newsletters.

A Few More Definitions

Beta

Beta is an indicator of volatility. I look for stocks whose price doesn't fluctuate too drastically. For example, AT&T has a beta of 0.21. The best way to understand this is if the S&P 500 moves up or down by 1 percent, this stock will only rise or fall by 0.21 percent.[22]

P/E Ratio (Price/Earnings Ratio)

This ratio is basically a measure of the multiple of earnings investors are willing to pay for a stock. It is the price of the stock divided by the earnings per share of stock.

PEG

This tells us whether or not the stock is expensive. It is calculated by the price/earnings ratio divided by the expected earnings growth rate. Yahoo Finance usually shows this on the Statistics page.

ROE (Return on Equity)

This shows how effectively the company uses the resources (assets) at its disposal. It can do one of four things with this money. It can pay a dividend, reduce debt, do a stock buyback, or reinvest in the company (e.g., through a new facility). The higher the number, the more effective the company is at increasing the return on investment.

Dividend

The money the company chooses to pay its stockholders throughout the year.

Payout Ratio

Ideally, this should be less than 75 percent or even less than 50 percent. This tells me if the company has enough cash from operations to pay me my dividend.

50-day Moving Average is Above 200-day Moving Average

This tells me the stock is in an uptrend.

Debt-to-Equity Ratio

This ratio provides a simple way for you to determine if a company has too much debt. It is shown on the Statistics page on Yahoo Finance. You want this ratio to be low, showing the company has enough cash to cover the debt.

Balance Sheet

This financial statement is made up of the assets the company owns and the liabilities it owes. Assets are recorded in order of liquidity, and liabilities are recorded in order of maturity (when they have to be repaid). This is similar to a person's net worth at a particular point in time.

Book Value of a Stock

Total assets minus total liabilities divided by total number of shares outstanding. If this equation is less than 1.00, you are essentially buying assets for pennies on the dollar. If it is greater than 1.00, you are paying more than the net worth of the company's assets. This can be good information for stock comparisons.

Section 31 Transaction Fee

When selling a stock, a fee imposed by the SEC to cover supervising and regulating the securities markets and securities professionals. This fee is usually passed on by the organization through which you buy/sell stocks. It is generally quite small and could change depending on the volume of transactions. (I tend to see it at around $6 per sale).

Following are 2 blank checklists for you to fill in your own information on a stock.

Rule Breaker Stock Examples	
Stock Name	
Symbol	
Market cap of > 7 billion	
Source	
Business/Emphasis	
Price Today	

	Plus	Minus	Sonja's Notes
Share Price > $7.00			
Beta in comfort zone (around 1.00)			
P/E (12 or < is cheap)			
PEG (1.00 or < is cheap)			
Net Profit Margin of 10% or > (net income/sales)			
Sales growth of >25%			
Earnings growth of >25%			
Positive cash flow (yes or no)			
52 week stock price lo to hi (not at hi)			
50 week moving average above 200 day moving average			
Insider holdings >10% but <50%			
Dividend (yes or no)			
Dividend amount 3% or > is great			
Payout ratio =<75%			

Rule Maker Stock Examples			
Stock Name			
Symbol			
Market cap of > 7 billion			
Source			
Business/Emphasis			
Price Today			

	Plus	Minus	Sonja's Notes
P/E (12 or < is cheap)			
PEG (1.00 or < is cheap)			
ROE (18 or > is great)			
Beta in comfort zone (around 1.00)			
50 day moving average above 200 day moving average			
52 week stock price lo to hi (not at hi)			
Sales growth of >10%			
Net Profit Margin of 10% or > (net income/sales)			
Gross margin >50% (gross income/gross sales)			
Current ratio > or =2.1			
Cash King Margin >10% (free cash flow/sales)			
Dividend (yes or no)			
Dividend amount 3% or more is great			
Payout ratio =<75%			
Foolish Flow Ratio =<1.25 current assets-cash/current liabilities-short term debt (efficient use of capital) found in balance sheet			

Websites

OXFORDCLUB.COM
Source of financial newsletters and trading services.

WALL STREET JOURNAL
Financial Newspaper

LIBERTYTHROUGHWEALTH.COM
User-friendly financial website.

WEALTHYRETIREMENT.COM
Financial Calculators

THEMOTLEYFOOL.COM
Online Financial Newsletter

MORNINGSTAR.COM
Financial Website

STANSBERRY RESEARCH/RETIREMENTMILLIONAIRE.COM
Financial newsletter written by a medical doctor and former investment professional that includes health and money-saving information; definitely not just for retirees.

Acknowledgements

I am indebted to many people for their help with this book. First and foremost, my in-laws Aline and Fredryc Haggert, without whom I would never have had the courage to invest. Thanks for your encouragement and introduction to The Oxford Club. Don't hesitate to send us some heavenly advice with our investments.

Thanks to Alex Green and Marc Lichtenfield of the Oxford Club for teaching me about investing. Because of what I learned from your newsletters, (*The Oxford club Communique* and *The Oxford Income Letter),* and books (The *Gone Fishin' Portfolio* and *Get Rich With Dividends*). I wanted to write this book for all those folks, like me, who need some help with the basics of investing. A special shout out to Steven King (no, not that one) of the Oxford Club, for helping Brian and I have fun with our investments. Your trips are the BEST!

A huge thank you to my beta readers; Donna Huston Murray, author of numerous mystery novels (donnahustonmurray.com), Elaine Pendrak, MD, Marilyn Long, (Marilyn Long, Designer) Elena Sickles CFP (Edward Jones), Sue DePaul, Joyce Goldberg, and Adriane Berg (author of "HOW NOT TO GO BROKE AT 102") and BIZ-TALK RADIO. You gave me such incredible suggestions!

A huge thanks to my husband, Brian, who was with me, every step of the way in our investing adventures and the writing of this book. Really hate to take all the credit (not really) because I wrote it. You are my biggest cheerleader who gives me professional critiques and great perspectives. I love our heated discussions about our investments; I always learn so much from you!

Endnotes

1   I am referring to an example here, not making any statements about tax policy or individual circumstances. You must check with your tax adviser.

2   IRS information.

3   http://www.investmentu.com/article/detail/46657/american-dream-how-to-become-millionaire-by-saving-190-dollars#.WdI6BmhSzD4

4   Taken from Oxford Club literature: {http://www.investmentu.com/content/detail/asset-allocation-model}

5   A number of articles all part of #5 in Chapter 5 Huang, Dr., George. "Mutual Funds are for Suckers." 17 July 2009 https://growthstockwire.com :Green, Alexander. "Your Mutual Fund is a Dog." Investment U, 15 June 2015: Issue 2561.

6   Kehm, Brian. "Are you paying more for Lesser Returns?" *Investment U* 27 May 2017 https://InvestmentU.com

7   Hulbert, Mark. "The 2016 Newsletter Honor Roll." The Hulbert Financial Digest Dec. 2015: Volume 36 Issue 4.

8   Yahoo Finance screenshot is for information purposes only. Not present day information.

9   Yahoo Finance screenshot is for information purposes only. Not present day information.

10   Data is from June 14, 2018.

11   The asset allocation model is taken from Oxford Club Literature.

12   Dividend Reinvestment Calculators are all from http://wealthyretirement.com/dividend-reinvestment-calculator

13 Washington Post, April 25, 2015, https://www.washingtonpost.com/business/get-there/the-remarkable-life-and-lessons-of-ronald-read/2015/04/24/7c12a26a-e944-11e4-9a6a-c1ab95a0600b_story.html?noredirect=on&utm_term=.52155034c6c5

14 Tim McAleenan, Jr., "Fidelity's Best Investors are Dead." The Conservative Investor, 26 May 2015. http://theconservativeincomeinvestor.com/2015/05/26/fidelitys-best-investors-are-dead/

15 Ibid

16 Clements, Jonathan. "Confused by Investing? Maybe It's the New Math." The Wall Street Journal 20 February 1996: Getting Going.

17 Hussman, John. The Business Insider, November 2013.

18 Patton, Mike. *Forbes*. "Is There a Problem Brewing in The Stock Market." 24 June 2014.

19 From a posting on the CNN Money Site. 28 July 2014.

20 USA Today, Money Section. "Stock Plunge Digs Deeper."

21 https://www.investopedia.com/terms/c/cpa.asp

22 Eifrig, David Jr. Stansberry Research, *Retirement Millionaire*, November 2014.

Bibliography

Blodget, Henry. "Be Prepared for Stocks to Crash 40-55%." Business Insider 9 Nov. 2013 < https://BusinessInsider.com>

Browning, E. S. "A Cliché a Day Keeps Wall Street Losses Away." The Wall Street Journal 27 December 2005: sec. C: 1.

Clemens, Jonathan. "Confused by Investing? Maybe it's the New Math." The Wall Street Journal 20 Feb. 1996: Getting Going.

Eversole, Brett. "Your Retirement Account Could be Costing You Millions." Steve Sjuggerud's Daily Wealth 22 July 2013.

"Exchange Traded Funds." (ETF) Investopedia. 14 July 2017 <https://investo-pedia.com>

Ferris, Dan. "If You're Worried about Gov't, Taxes or Interest Rates, Read This." Steve Sjuggerud's Daily Wealth 30 Oct. 2013.

Finance. Morningstar June 14, 2018 <morningstar.com>

Finance. Yahoo 25 May 2016 <https://yahoo.com>

Gardner, David and Tom. The Motley Fool Investment Workbook. New York: Simon and Schuster, 2003: 109-111.

Green, Alexander. "Why Your Mutual Fund is a Dog." Investment U 15 June 2015: Issue 2561: chapter five.

Green, Alexander. "How to Become Financially Independent." The Oxford Club Communique 1 Aug. 2012: page ten.

Huang, Dr., George. "Mutual Funds are for Suckers." 17 July 2009 <https://growthstockwire.com>

Hulbert, Mark. "The 2016 Newsletter Honor Roll." The Hulbert Financial Digest Dec. 2015: Volume 36 Issue four.

Katzeff, Paul. "How to Evaluate a Financial Adviser." Women's Wall Street 3 Dec. 2004.

Kehm, Brian. "Are You Paying More for Lesser Returns?" Investment U 27 May 2017 <https://Investmentu.com>

Lichtenfeld, Marc. "Get Rich with Dividends. Hoboken, N. J.: John Wiley and Sons, 2012.

Lichtenfeld, Marc. "The Most Important Thing You Should Do to Make Money in 2015." Investment U. 21 Jan. 2015 <https://InvestmentU.com>

Lichtenfeld, Marc. "Want Your Kids to be Rich? Do This." The Oxford Club Communique 1 May 2013.

Lichtenfeld, Marc. "Three Easy Steps to Beat the 'Wall Street Casino'." The Oxford Club Communique 17 April 2017.

McAleenan Jr. "Fidelity's Best Investors are Dead." The Conservative Income Investor 26 May 2015.

McDonald, Steve. "The Harsh Truth About Women and Finances." Wealthy Retirement 25 April 2017 < https://InvestmentU.com>

McDonald, Steve. 'Slap in the Face" Award: Stock Mutual Funds and the Advisers Who Love Them' Investment U Conference 2015 22 February 2015

Ritholz, Barry. "The Remarkable Life and Lessons of the $8 Million Dollar Janitor." The Washington Post 25 April 2015.

Rooney, Ben. "Psychics are Bullish on Stocks." CNN Money. 28 July 2014 <https://money.cnn.com>

Russell, Richard. "Rich Man, Poor Man." Dow Theory Letters http://www.dailyp-fennig.com/special-bonus-edition-9/

Shell, Adam and Strauss, Gary. "Stock Plunge Digs Deeper." USA Today, US Edition 15 Jan. 2015 <https:// pressreader.com/USA/USAToday>

"S & P Return Calculator with Dividend Reinvestment." 13 July 2017: 9:45 AM <https://DQYDJ.com>

"Stock." Business Dictionary. <https://www.Businessdictionary.com> 12 July 2017.

About the Author

Sonja Haggert is a veteran of various sales and marketing positions. She spent the majority of her career at Met-Pro Corporation, becoming vice president of the corporation and general manager of the Keystone Filter Division.

During her career, she was a contributor to numerous trade publications, including providing chapters for two books published by Richard D. Irwin, Inc., now a part of McGraw-Hill Publishing. This love of writing led to a second career in retirement as a business writer and editor.

Sonja is on the board of Laurel House, a nonprofit working to end domestic violence. During her time there, she has served in numerous capacities, including co-president. At present, she is a Laurel House vice president and is active on many committees, including her role as chair of the investment committee.

Sonja and her husband, Brian, were instrumental in developing and formalizing the board of directors for Let's Go Play, a nonprofit for children with autism spectrum disorder.

Sonja has a BS in business administration from Villanova University. She lives with Brian in suburban Philadelphia.